*Day Place, Co. Kerry*

# Maynooth Studies in Local History

SERIES EDITOR Michael Potterton

You are reading one of the six volumes in the Maynooth Studies in Local History (MSLH) series for 2023. A benefit of being the editor of this series is the early opportunity to read a very wide variety of bite-sized histories covering events and activities from the magnificent to the outrageous in every nook and cranny of this remarkable island. This year's offerings take us from Bronze Age burials in west Kerry to a three-year dairy war in 1930s east Donegal, via an entrepreneur extraordinaire from late Georgian Cork, a revelatory survey of dire poverty in pre-Famine Westmeath, a century of exclusive terrace-life in colourful Tralee and the complex social networks of a family of Francophile Catholic landed gentry from Kildare. Together, these six studies take us on an astonishing journey on which we encounter smugglers, umbrella makers, lifelike automata, difficult marriage- and education choices, resolute defiance, agrarian violence, rapidly changing religious and political landscapes and a petition to have a region transferred from one nation to another.

These half-a-dozen volumes show how the 'local' focus of a *local history* can range from an individual person (Marsden Haddock) to a family (the Mansfields), a street (Day Place), a village (Portmagee), a county (Donegal and Westmeath) and beyond. The six authors have taken their stories from relative obscurity to centre stage. Denis Casey now joins Terence Dooley as one of only two people to have published three volumes in this series (though they are set to be joined by a third in 2024!).

This year in the Department of History at Maynooth University we are celebrating seventy years of excellence in teaching, research and publication (1953–2023) and we are especially delighted to be relaunching our enormously successful MA in Local History. Theses from this programme have traditionally provided the backbone of the MSLH series and we look forward to another rich crop in the years to come.

Whether you ask Alexa, ChatGPT or Raymond Gillespie, there is no doubting that Local History is valuable and significant. AI has evolved considerably since I grew up on a dairy farm in south Co. Meath and it is sure to play an increasing role in the research, writing and dissemination of local history. As with so many new technologies, of course, the greatest challenge is perhaps going to be maximizing the potential of Artificial Intelligence without compromising the integrity of the results.

*Maynooth Studies in Local History: Number 164*

# Day Place, Co. Kerry
## 'The most respectable locality in Tralee'

Laurence Jones

FOUR COURTS PRESS

Set in 11.5pt on 13.5pt Bembo by
Carrigboy Typesetting Services for
FOUR COURTS PRESS LTD
7 Malpas Street, Dublin 8, Ireland
www.fourcourtspress.ie
*and in North America for*
FOUR COURTS PRESS
c/o IPG, 814 N Franklin Street, Chicago, IL 60610

ISBN 978-1-80151-097-4

Printed in Ireland
by SprintPrint, Dublin

# Contents

# Acknowledgments

In Tralee: Mike Lynch, the county archivist, and Helen O'Carroll, curator of the Kerry County Museum and a mine of Tralee-based nuggets of information. Also, Victoria McCarthy, architectural heritage officer with Kerry County Council, whose enthusiasm for Day Place is unbounded. She has very kindly kept me 'in the loop' on the major restoration project, which happened to coincide with my research. I could not forget Canon Jim Stephens, rector of Tralee, who literally locked me into the church to spend hours examining the memorials. Also, Gerald O'Carroll, next to whom I found myself squashed into a pew and who happily had a spare copy of his book with him.

In Dublin: Sophie Evans, assistant librarian at the Royal Irish Academy, Robert Gallagher, library administrator at the Representative Church Body Library, Dolores Grant, archivist at the National Archives of Ireland, Stephen Nolan of the Valuation Office and various officers and administrators at the National Library of Ireland, the General Registrar's Office and the Irish Architectural Archive. At University College Cork: Drs Donal Ó Drisceoil, Rachel Murphy and Andy Bielenberg.

I would like to dedicate this work to the memory of Russell McMorran, who died during the writing of it. Although I never had the opportunity to meet him, he was by all accounts a walking encyclopaedia of Tralee history and folklore, and without the breadcrumbs he left, I would never have found the trails to follow.

# Introduction

While Tralee has medieval origins, nothing remains from that period except street plans and place-names. A map published in 1756 shows a small town with rivers running through its streets. The map is dedicated to Sir Thomas Denny and much of its area is covered by the landscaped gardens of Tralee Castle, then seat of the Dennys.[1]

The Dennys had gained Tralee after the Desmond Rebellion. The town was incorporated as a borough in 1613 under the control of the family (see ch. 3). However, Tralee barely developed, with little investment by the Dennys except in their castle and demesne.

Enter Robert Day. He was the son of the chancellor of Ardfert and was born near Tralee. Day was a member of parliament for Ardfert and a king's counsel. In 1795 his daughter Elizabeth married Sir Edward Denny, third baronet. Under the marriage settlement, he became the principal trustee of the Denny family estates. Within a few years the Dennys left Kerry for England and Day was managing Tralee on their behalf. In 1798 he became a justice of the court of king's bench and was invariably known as Mr Justice Day from then on. He set about improving the town. In June 1801 his nephew obtained the lease of the area known as 'The Lawn' from Letitia Blennerhassett.[2] Day seems to have been the instigator and it was recalled the 'plot was purchased ... for £100'.[3] Certainly it was he who divided the site into building plots, which he was selling by 1803. He was already building no. 2 and the leases stipulated that the lessees build good, slated dwelling houses 'conformable in every respect as to uniformity of the front' with his own house within three years. The latest of these leases in the Registry of Deeds is dated September 1811.[4]

The ten houses are impressive. Three storeys over a basement with two parlours on the ground floor and three large bedrooms and a drawing room on the upper floors. The basement served as a kitchen and servants' quarters.[5] Their exteriors were finished in an elegant classical style with limestone steps and door casings and fanlights over

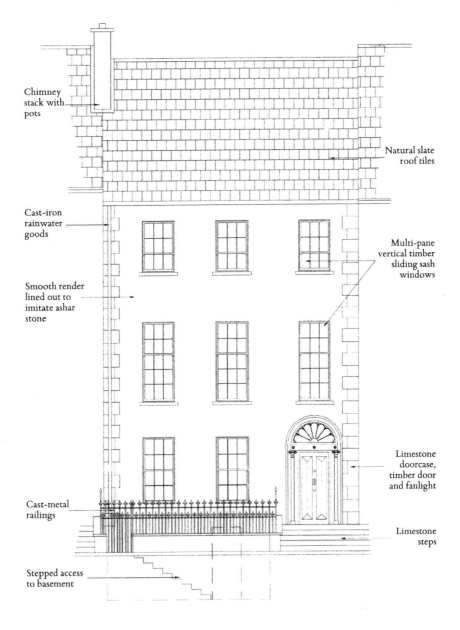

Chimney stack with pots

Natural slate roof tiles

Cast-iron rainwater goods

Multi-pane vertical timber sliding sash windows

Smooth render lined out to imitate ashar stone

Limestone doorcase, timber door and fanlight

Cast-metal railings

Limestone steps

Stepped access to basement

1. Typical Day Place front elevation (JCA Architects, with permission)

**2.** Early twentieth-century postcard of Day Place. The contrast between the working-class women and children outside the railing and the respectable men inside is striking (Muckross House Library, Trustees of Muckross House (Killarney) CLG)

the front doors (fig. 1). Bespoke iron railings and gates separated the entry to the basement from the flagged pavement. The long narrow rear yards had private wells, stables and coach houses opening onto a rear lane. These houses were unlike anything in Tralee and echoed developments in Dublin and Limerick. The terrace, known as Day's Buildings, Day's Place, Day-Place and eventually Day Place, was home to some of the wealthiest and most influential inhabitants of the area.

The aim of this book is to examine the occupants of the ten houses over the period of a hundred years, from 1830 to 1930. This was a time of enormous political and economic change both locally and nationally. By studying the select group living in the houses we will see any changes that reflect these transformations, including religious affiliation, political allegiance and sources of income.

As the residents were prominent, they left evidence of their activities above and beyond the basic records generated by the lives of the general population. Time and space allow only a selection of Day Place residents to be discussed in detail. Examples are given in three thematic chapters about commerce, religion and local government. The appendix gives a brief list of the identifiable householders of Day Place from about 1830 to 1930.

# 1. 'Many of the dealers are wealthy'

The retail trade of Tralee is an extensive and improving one; and many of the dealers are wealthy.[1]

So wrote the Scottish travel writer Henry David Inglis, who visited the town in 1834. There had been much progress in the commercial life of the town since the beginning of the century. In 1808 Tralee had 'no manufactories of consequence' and the shallow depth of the bay would 'not admit of vessels of 40 or 50 tons to come nearer than 1 mile of the town'.[2] Inglis stated that twenty years before his visit 'Tralee was little else than a congregation of cabins; and within a far shorter period, it has received, as a merchant of the town expressed it, its new face'.[3]

Over the study period, several of the houses in Day Place had heads of household who described themselves as 'merchants'. This term included two different kinds of capitalist: those involved in the milling and shipping businesses and those who owned or managed retail outlets. The purpose of this chapter is to discover what evidence exists as to the changes in the economy of Tralee and how this is reflected in the wealthy merchant class of the terrace.

## 'A CONSIDERABLE BUSINESS IS DONE IN FLOUR, GRAIN, BACON, BUTTER': THE EXPORTERS AND IMPORTERS OF TRALEE

By the beginning of the nineteenth century agriculture was altering from pastoral to tillage farming, a shift taking place throughout Ireland. In 1811 the countryside around Tralee was described as 'particularly fertile and, in general, well cultivated; supplying not only its own population with corn, potatoes, butter &c. but making very considerable exports of those articles of general consumption'.[4] In 1824 *Pigot's directory* noted that 'Corn is the principle article of exportation, which has within the last twelve years increased in an unexampled degree'.[5]

Inglis tells us:

> Since the year 1825, the corn export trade of Tralee has increased
> about one-third; and the home trade about one-fifth. The butter
> export trade of Tralee used to be considerable; but it is greatly
> on the decline, scarcely one-twentieth part of the quantity being
> now exported, comparatively with the year 1825.[6]

The growth of the export trade of grain was confirmed by Samuel
Lewis in 1837:

> About 15 years since the export of grain was confined to two or
> three small cargoes annually; there is now a considerable export,
> which is increasing every year; the chief articles are wheat and
> oats ... butter is also exported, but not to its former extent: coal
> and timber are the chief articles imported.[7]

An examination of the 'Port News' in the *Kerry Evening Post* for
the period provides corroboration. In May 1831 the *Clyde* sailed for
Liverpool with 540 barrels of wheat and 155 of barley while the *Anne*
carried 720 barrels of oats.[8] Imports consisted largely of timber from
New Brunswick and Quebec, iron from south Wales and assorted
items such as rock salt and soap from Liverpool.[9]

### FROM BLENNERVILLE TO THE BASIN

The busy port that appears in these descriptions was not in Tralee
but at Blennerville, about a mile from the town. This purpose-built
settlement was established in the mid-eighteenth century by the
Blennerhassett family. Large ships could not navigate the various
inlets of the River Lee that penetrated the heart of Tralee and the
construction of quays at the river's mouth at Blennerville served these
vessels. The Blennerhassetts also constructed a windmill to grind the
grain. The census reports of 1821 and 1831 refer to Blennerville as
having 'an extensive corn trade carried on with Liverpool'.[10]

In 1828 a group of local businessmen banded together to put
an act through parliament to construct a ship canal leading from
Blennerville to a basin on the edge of the town. The act describes the

purpose of the new port in some detail, saying it would be of 'general benefit' and specifically:

> facilitating the export of corn, butter, flour, beef, pork, linen, cattle, kelp, the importation of timber, iron, salt, tea, sugars, wines, and other articles connected with the improving trade of … Tralee, and would tend to the promotion of agriculture and fisheries as also the employment of the poor.[11]

This was the first time the emerging merchant class had been given any formal power or part in local administration. The act created a Board of Harbour Commissioners, which was to include anyone who had subscribed thirty pounds towards the construction of the canal and was empowered to fill any vacancies in its membership.

Work began in 1832 but coincided with a cholera epidemic. In 1836 all works ceased and there was uncertainty until the Board of Works assumed control in 1840 and construction resumed in 1841. It was to take another five years and three contractors before the Board of Works were able to pass the completed canal and basin to the Tralee Harbour Commissioners in April 1846.[12]

The canal had its critics even before it was finished: 'A ship canal is now constructing from the bay to the town; but its probable utility is doubted by many. It is thought that the strong westerly gales which blow into the bay will accumulate sand in the canal', was the verdict of the *Parliamentary Gazetteer* in 1844.[13]

### FROM THE BASIN TO FENIT

Only ships of shallow draught could use the canal. Larger vessels had to moor off Great Samphire Island in the north of Tralee Bay with goods being transhipped to smaller vessels. The delays and possible damage to cargoes soon made the canal, which was prone to silting, impractical.

Railways reached Tralee, after many delays, in 1859. In 1879 a public meeting was held in Tralee Courthouse. Those attending included the chairman and members of Tralee Town Commissioners, the parish priest, magistrates, bank managers and the principal merchants of the town. The meeting investigated the possibility of building a railway from Tralee to a new deep-water port at Fenit, where a pier would be built. It was claimed the trade of Tralee was declining and that the government was likely to lend money to create employment for those constructing the line.[14] The idea was adopted, and parliamentary approval quickly obtained.[15] Thus was constituted an entirely new body, the Tralee and Fenit Pier and Harbour Commissioners.

The make-up of the new board was markedly different from that created in 1828, reflecting changes in both government and trade. There were two *ex-officio* members from bodies that had not existed fifty-two years earlier: the chairmen of the Tralee Board of Guardians and of the Tralee Town Commissioners. The Board of Trade (a central government body based in London) appointed a commissioner. Three directors or shareholders of the Tralee and Fenit Railway Company were to become commissioners. The users of the port were represented by the 'two persons who shall have paid dues on the largest number of tons, not less than five thousand tons, of merchandise imported or exported … into or from the harbour' in the previous year and three commissioners elected by those who paid dues on two thousand tons and upwards of merchandise imported.

For eight years there were two rival bodies of commissioners. In 1887 the railway to Fenit was opened and in the following year the ship canal was vested in the Tralee and Fenit commissioners and gave them jurisdiction over all landing places in Tralee Bay.[16] The canal and basin, seen as vital to the town's prosperity forty years earlier, quickly fell into disrepair.

### SHIP OWNERS, GRAIN MERCHANTS AND MILLERS IN DAY PLACE

*The Palmers of no. 2 Day Place*

In May 1851 Letitia Rowan, occupant of no. 2 Day Place, died. The inscription 'Mrs Letitia Rowan' appears at the head of the entry in the Valuation Office *House Book*, but a line has been drawn through it and the name 'John Palmer' written in a different hand. As the valuations of this part of Tralee were completed in December 1851, this pinpoints the arrival of Palmer during the latter part of the year.[17] Palmer was a miller and grain dealer and the proprietor of Bunnow Mills about 16km east of Tralee.[18] He arrived in Kerry from Galway in

about 1843.[19] He took over an existing facility, as Samuel Lewis noted
that at 'Bunnow there is a large flour-mill' in 1837.[20] In 1853 there
was a crisis in the Town Commission (see ch. 3). An extraordinary
meeting was called following the resignation of the chairman and
two commissioners and questions over the 'financial condition' of
the board. Palmer was one of three new commissioners who were co-
opted to fill the vacancies.[21]

John Palmer died at no. 2 Day Place on St Stephen's Day 1860.[22]
The *Tralee Chronicle* said that since his arrival in Kerry, Palmer had
'sustained a commercial character of the highest order, and was much
esteemed by all who knew him'. The newspaper also noted that
he 'has left a wife and six children, but, we are happy to say, with
ample means'.[23] Henrietta Palmer, widow of John, continued the
milling business.[24] By 1870 she was included in the 'Nobility, Gentry
& Clergy' section of *Slater's directory*.[25] She vacated no. 2 Day Place
in 1876, leaving her eldest son, Richard Elliott Palmer, as head of
household.[26] She retired to England, where she died in 1908. She was
buried alongside her husband in a grand tomb in the New Cemetery,
Tralee.[27]

In June 1878 a fire broke out in the mill at Bunnow, which was
'totally destroyed'.[28] In the following month Palmer invited tenders
for the rebuilding of the mills.[29] Although admitted to fill a vacancy
on the Town Commission in 1877, he seems to have had little interest
in Tralee or the family business, instead spending the 'ample means'
his father had left.[30] In June 1882 he offered the lease of no. 2 for sale.[31]
Dr John Mary Harrington (see ch. 3) took up residence in the house
in 1884.[32]

In 1885 Palmer moved to New York and Bunnow Mills were
offered for sale.[33] By 1893 the mills were in the ownership of Palmer's
brother-in-law and cousin and were advertised for sale.[34] Despite the
positive description in the advertisement, this was the end of milling
at Bunnow and the 25-inch Ordnance Survey map surveyed in the
following year describes the mill as 'disused'.[35]

## Richard Latchford

The Latchfords were a Palatine family, relocated to Co. Limerick in
1709.[36] Richard's father, John Latchford, arrived in 1829 in Tralee,
where he established a bakery. In 1843 he took over the corn mill

at Derrymore, 11km east of the town.[37] In 1867 Richard inherited
the family business, which by then had expanded to include mills
in Cahersiveen, Dingle and Listowel.[38] In 1871 he moved into no. 6
Day Place. The 1870s was a decade of expansion and modernization
of the Latchford businesses. Modern iron ships were purchased, and
a complex of warehouses built close to the basin. The Latchfords
quickly outgrew Day Place both physically (they had eight children)
and socially (large villas to the north of the town were becoming a
mark of social status). In 1879 they removed themselves to the select
suburb of Oakpark about 1km out of the town.[39] The Latchford
business empire is better recorded than that of the Palmers. A five-
storey steam-powered mill was built adjacent to the rail terminus in
1887.[40] A limited company from 1903, the firm expanded into animal-
feed production and hardware retail before finally closing in the early
1980s.[41]

### J.W. Steele: trouble at the mill

Latchford's was one of three large family businesses that dominated
Tralee in the early years of the twentieth century. The others were
Kellihers and Donovans. Donovans were the largest employers in
the town. By 1905 the business was in financial difficulties and in
December a limited company was formed with R. & H. Hall of Cork
taking a controlling interest.[42] The changed regime introduced a new
family to Day Place. In 1906 John William Steele arrived in Tralee and
was living in no. 8 by 1907. Although he described himself as a grain
merchant, he was in fact managing director of Donovans Ltd.[43] As the
company was one of the five largest importers, they were entitled to
nominate a member to the Tralee and Fenit Pier and Harbour Board.
Steele attended his first meeting in this capacity in June 1908 and took
an active role in the board's discussions. During much of this time the
board was chaired by Richard Latchford.[44]

Steele's fortunes rose and fell with those of the company. In 1913
Hall's overhauled the loss-making company, with directors' salaries
halved and a reduction in the size of the workforce.[45] The Steele
family vanished from Kerry in November 1915.[46] The departure of
Steele ended a period of sixty years of grain merchants, importers
and exporters living at Day Place. The nature of the businesses had
changed. Slightly chaotic family businesses and inherited money had

been replaced by a harder management style. Steam power replaced water power and modern port facilities with increased regulation were established. While some of the companies were to continue to operate and diversify, their proprietors no longer desired to live in a Georgian town house but preferred the seaside or rural villa.

'A VERY ABUNDANT EXHIBITION OF ALL KINDS OF MANUFACTURED
GOODS, AND APPAREL; AND EVERY SHOP IN THE TOWN WAS CROWDED
TO THE DOOR'

Inglis's description of the shops of Tralee in 1834 illustrates a change in the nature of commerce in the town.[47] There was still street trading going on in 1837 according to Lewis, as there were 'no regular marketplaces, and the dealings are carried on in the public streets, to the great inconvenience of the inhabitants'.[48] The new shops that replaced the street traders were remarked upon in 1852: 'new shops with new plate glass fronts in their windows – new flag ways under foot and new light (gas light we mean) over head'.[49]

Large business premises were built along the Mall and Castle Street in what became the shopping district of Tralee. These three- or four-storey terraced houses were purpose-built with a lower level exclusively for retail use and upper levels as residences.[50] Advertisements in the local press give an idea of the goods and services now being offered. An example is the *Kerry Evening Post* of 5 November 1881. A single page carries advertisements for seven businesses in the area. These comprise drapery, millinery, dress-making and tailoring, paint and glass, upholstering, cabinet making, coffin manufacture and farm machinery. There is an emphasis on both retail and wholesale, low prices and 'home manufacture'.[51]

### Michael B. Stokes: 'honest work and business pluck'

Patrick Stokes established a 'Distillery Stores and Tobacco and Snuff Manufactory' in 1854.[52] He imported and sold tobacco and established a pipe factory.[53] The Port News in the *Tralee Chronicle* showed the size of the business by April 1857. In that month Stokes is shown as having three hogsheads of tobacco imported and placed in bonded warehouses and 577 pounds of tobacco removed from bond. Stokes became a Town Commissioner in the 1860s.[54] He died in 1878.[55]

The business was inherited by his son, Michael Benjamin Stokes. Michael B. Stokes married in February 1881 and soon after moved to no. 5 Day Place.[56] Like his father, he became a Town Commissioner, and was described as a 'consistent and sterling Nationalist all his life' who supported the Land League and National League.[57] In 1886 he was sworn on to the grand jury of the county, at which point he proposed a resolution calling on the government to halt evictions.[58]

An advertisement dated April 1888 appeared in the local press advertising no. 5 for lease.[59] It appears that Stokes moved to his business premises at The Square. He certainly died there on 9 June 1900.[60] This was not the end of the Stokes family's association with the terrace. Margaret Stokes, his wife, returned to Day Place in 1898.[61] She came back to the street, but to a different house, no. 7. By the time of the 1901 census she was a widow. In the ten-room house she lived with a domestic servant and a guest, a 27-year-old governess.[62] She did not survive until the next year, dying of heart failure at no. 7 on 29 December.[63]

## The Barretts: a dynasty of shopkeepers

Denis Barrett was a grocer and wine merchant. He was the son of a farmer and moved to Tralee in the 1870s. By July 1878 he was living in Bridge Street when he married Mary Anne Riordan. He was described as a shopkeeper and his wife as a shopkeeper's daughter from The Mall.[64]

In 1887 the family moved into no. 6 Day Place; another example of the Catholic merchant class moving from 'over the shop'. Involved in Nationalist politics, he was nominated for election to the Town Commission more than once, but never gained a seat. By 1896 Barrett's health was failing and he surrendered the liquor licence for his premises at Lower Bridge Street.[65] He died at Day Place in March 1897 aged 48.[66] Shortly after his death there was an auction that showed both his wealth and his interests. Among the items offered for sale were a seaside lodge in the Spa area, horses, carriages and carts, dairy cows and equipment.[67]

Mary Anne Barrett, like Henrietta Palmer, was a formidable entrepreneur in her own right. She continued the grocery business at Bridge Street. She vacated Day Place in 1906, and there was an auction of high-class furniture at no. 6 in May of that year.[68] Like

other residents of Day Place, she advanced to a substantial house
in the rural surroundings of Tralee.[69] As well as being the home for
members of the Barrett family and servants, it was used as business
accommodation and six clerks were listed as living there in 1911.[70] No.
6 was retained by the Barrett family who made numerous attempts to
let out the house. It was frequently vacant, however.

Timothy Barrett inherited the family business. In 1909 he married
Frances, the daughter of John Walsh, in a lavish ceremony at
Killarney Cathedral.[71] Walsh was a draper with his business premises
in The Square and had just moved into no. 8 at the time of the
marriage. One can speculate as to how the newlyweds met, but the
next development can surely be no coincidence. Barrett advertised
the sale of the premises in Bridge Street in March 1917 and it was
acquired by his father-in-law and his brother, who then traded as
Walsh Brothers.[72] No. 6 also featured as a lot in the auction but did
not sell. Barrett eventually disposed of the house in a separate sale in
December 1917.[73]

*John P. Dooley and James Hoffman, managers of 'The Munster Cash'*

No. 10 was occupied in turn by the two general managers of the
Munster Cash Company. The company opened its department store
at The Mall in 1881.[74] John Dooley, who was the occupant from 1880,
was the first manager of the innovative new business.[75] He remained
there for about five years. Dooley left the management of the
Munster Cash and set up in business himself at 5 Denny Street, over
the road from his former employers. In March 1885 he advertised that
he would be opening on 11 April with an 'entirely new, carefully
selected and well-assorted stock of millinery, mantles, costumes,
flowers, feathers, dress material, tweeds, coatings, trouserings, hats,
shirts, ties &co. &co.'[76]

On 25 August the contents of no. 10 Day Place were auctioned as
Dooley was 'removing to his Business House in Denny Street'.[77] The
next part of the Dooley story raises suspicions. On 4 September 1885
the second floor of his premises at Denny Street was destroyed by
fire. He was away from home at the time.[78] The part of the building
damaged consisted of the stock rooms for his business and after being
awarded £900 by insurance companies he went to Dublin to seek
the protection of the bankruptcy court. In November, testimony

was given to the court that he had not since returned to Tralee or communicated with his wife, and his whereabouts were unknown.[79] No more is heard of him until his death in New York in 1907. The death notice explained that he 'went to America some years ago, where he occupied a lucrative position in the wholesale drapery trade'.[80]

The Valuation Office revision books show no. 10 Day Place as having been vacant in 1886 but in 1888 it was occupied by James Hoffman.[81] An 1892 guide to the south of Ireland includes an advertisement for the Munster Cash Company, which mentions Hoffman by name:

> An efficient staff of about fifty sales assistants and work hands is engaged in the various departments under the competent control of Mr Hoffman, the courteous manager of the firm, whose unremitting efforts are constantly exercised in maintaining the systematic order and organisation necessary in the conduct of an establishment of this extent and importance.[82]

In 1897 Hoffman, like Dooley before him, left the employment of Munster Cash and set up his own drapery business.[83] Hoffman only lived at Day Place for about two years – the house was once again vacant in 1890.[84] He had a large family and moved to a newly built house on the edge of Tralee.[85] By 1911 he was able to afford to live in the fashionable Spa area.[86] The family's Palatine origins are confirmed by both the surname and the fact that their religion was returned as Methodist in the census forms.

# 2. Day Place: religious affiliation and conflict

This chapter explores the religious make-up of Tralee over the period and the heads of household in Day Place. It concludes by looking at some religious controversies related to the street involving prominent residents who actively promoted the Methodist and Catholic denominations. In this way, one can see how representative the population of Day Place was of the wider area and the changes in the power and influence of religious groups as emancipation and secularization overturned the existing order.

We cannot be certain of the religious allegiance of the population of Tralee until the 1860s as it became included in the census returns only in 1861.[1] In that year the town had a population of slightly over 10,000. Almost nine out of ten people were Catholic and one out of ten were members of the established church. There were small numbers of Presbyterians and Methodists.[2] From 1871 the census reports organized religious profession in a slightly different way. With disestablishment, the 'Established Church' category was replaced with 'Protestant Episcopalian', in other words Church of Ireland. It also included a new category of 'All Other Denominations', which were not differentiated below county level.

Tralee's population remained a little below 10,000 in the years between 1871 and 1901.[3] Catholics increased their share of the town's population by about 2 per cent to 92 per cent. Numbers of adherents to the Church of Ireland steadily declined, with just 632 recorded in 1901 – less than 6.5 per cent of the population. The number of Methodists rose above one hundred in 1871 before falling away sharply in 1901 to eighty-three. The number of Presbyterians remained around fifty until 1901, when it rose to eighty-five.

Household schedules prior to the 1901 census have been destroyed, but there are ways to reconstruct the religious affiliation of the heads of household from the 1830s, if imperfectly. First, there is a list of voters made in 1831. It gives the names and addresses of the voters, their religion and who they cast their vote for.[4] It was not until 1872 that the secret ballot was introduced, although the religious information was added by the supporters of Morgan O'Connell. The list was printed as a poster after the election for all to see. Of the 174 registered voters in the borough of Tralee, six had addresses in Day Place. The relevant entries are tabulated below:

**Table 1. Religions of registered voters, Day Place, 1831**

| Name | Religion |
|---|---|
| Walter Hussey Esq. | Catholic |
| Nicholas King Esq. MD | Catholic |
| Rowland Blennerhassett Esq. | Protestant & Dissenters |
| Charles G. Fairfield Esq. DL | Protestant & Dissenters |
| George Hilliard Esq. | Protestant & Dissenters |
| Rowan Purdon Esq. MD | Protestant & Dissenters |

The list gives neither the house number nor the denomination of the Protestants. There are other sources that provide these details. All those included in the latter category were prominent members of the Established Church. While none of the valuation books or directories that identify the occupants of the street specifically list religion, the people involved are notable enough for this to be readily ascertained. With the censuses of 1901 and 1911 we have solid information. Table 2 summarizes the position from 1831 to 1891, while tables 3 and 4 provide more detailed information.

*Day Place*

**Table 2. Religions of heads of household, Day Place, 1831–91**

| Year | 1 | 2 | 3 | 4 | 5 |
|------|---|---|---|---|---|
| 1831 | Busteed NC | Fairfield EC | O'Connell RC | McGillycuddy EC | Hussey RC |
| 1841 | Busteed NC | Fairfield EC | Blennerhassett EC | McGillycuddy EC | Hussey RC |
| 1851 | Murphy RC | Rowan EC | Slattery RC | McGillycuddy EC | Hickson EC |
| 1861 | O'Callaghan RC | Palmer EC | Slattery RC | McGillycuddy EC | Crosbie EC |
| 1871 | O'Callaghan RC | Palmer EC | Slattery/Panormo RC & EC | McGillycuddy EC | Stokes EC |
| 1881 | O'Callaghan RC | Palmer EC | Lawlor EC | McGillycuddy EC | Barry RC |
| 1891 | Scott RC | Harrington RC | Moriarty EC | McGillycuddy EC | Moon EC |

| Year | 6 | 7 | 8 | 9 | 10 |
|------|---|---|---|---|----|
| 1831 | Blennerhassett EC | Ponsonby EC | King RC | Hilliard EC | Purdon EC |
| 1841 | Blennerhassett EC | Ponsonby EC | O'Connor EC | Hilliard EC | Day EC |
| 1851 | Blennerhassett EC | Ponsonby EC | Busteed NC | Hilliard EC | Day EC |
| 1861 | Purdon EC | Quill EC | Lawlor EC | Hilliard EC | Naughton RC |
| 1871 | Latchford EC | Quill EC | Lawlor EC | Sullivan RC | Maybury EC |
| 1881 | Leahy EC | Quill EC | Lawlor EC | Sullivan RC | Dooley RC |
| 1891 | Barrett RC | Quill EC | Morphy EC | VACANT | Conroy RC |

KEY:
EC = Established Church or Church of Ireland
RC = Roman Catholic
NC = Non-Conformist Protestants

At the 1901 census there were 73 persons recorded as living at nos 1–9, while no. 10 was unoccupied. Fifty-three were Catholic (RC), 18 Church of Ireland (Protestant Episcopalian – PE) and 2 were Presbyterian (P). The heads of household of six of the occupied houses were Catholic and the three remaining were Church of Ireland.

**Table 3.** Religious professions, Day Place, 1901 census

| Number | Persons | RC | PE | P | Notes |
|---|---|---|---|---|---|
| 1 | Head of Household & Family | 2 | - | - | A school: these were Catholic clergy acting as teachers |
| | Lodgers & Guests | - | - | - | |
| | Servants | 1 | - | - | |
| 2 | Head of Household & Family | 5 | - | - | |
| | Lodgers & Guests | - | - | - | |
| | Servants | 2 | - | - | |
| 3 | Head of Household & Family | 7 | - | - | |
| | Lodgers & Guests | - | - | - | |
| | Servants | 4 | 1 | - | |
| 4 | Head of Household & Family | - | 4 | - | |
| | Lodgers & Guests | - | 1 | - | |
| | Servants | 2 | 1 | - | |
| 5 | Head of Household & Family | - | 6 | - | |
| | Lodgers & Guests | - | - | 1 | |
| | Servants | 1 | - | - | |
| 6 | Head of Household & Family | 3 | - | - | |
| | Lodgers & Guests | 8 | - | - | 7 grocers' assistants (employees) were living in the property |
| | Servants | 2 | - | - | |
| 7 | Head of Household & Family | 1 | - | - | |
| | Lodgers & Guests | 1 | - | - | |
| | Servants | 1 | - | - | |
| 8 | Head of Household & Family | - | 5 | - | |
| | Lodgers & Guests | - | - | - | |
| | Servants | 1 | - | 2 | |
| 9 | Head of Household & Family | 6 | - | - | The Reynolds family were caretakers of the Tralee Catholic Literary Society which occupied much of the building |
| | Lodgers & Guests | - | - | - | |
| | Servants | - | - | - | |

**Table 4. Religious professions, Day Place, 1911 census**

| Number | Persons | RC | PE | Notes |
|---|---|---|---|---|
| 1 | Head of Household & Family | 1 | - | A school: a Catholic clergyman (the principal) lived on site |
|  | Lodgers & Guests | - | - | |
|  | Servants | 2 | - | |
| 2 | Head of Household & Family | 5 | - | |
|  | Lodgers & Guests | - | - | |
|  | Servants | 2 | - | |
| 3 | Head of Household & Family | 6 | - | |
|  | Lodgers & Guests | - | - | |
|  | Servants | 2 | - | |
| 4 | Head of Household & Family | 3 | - | |
|  | Lodgers & Guests | - | - | |
|  | Servants | 2 | - | |
| 5 | Head of Household & Family | - | 3 | |
|  | Lodgers & Guests | - | - | |
|  | Servants | 1 | - | |
| 8 | Head of Household & Family | 4 | - | |
|  | Lodgers & Guests | - | - | |
|  | Servants | 1 | - | |
| 9 | Head of Household & Family | 3 | - | The Phillips family were caretakers of the Tralee Catholic Literary Society |
|  | Lodgers & Guests | - | - | |
|  | Servants | - | - | |
| 10 | Head of Household & Family | 3 | - | |
|  | Lodgers & Guests | - | - | |
|  | Servants | 1 | - | |

At the 1911 census there were forty-five persons living in nos 1–10. Two houses (6 and 7) were unoccupied. Forty-two of the residents were Catholic and three were Church of Ireland. Just one house had a Protestant as head of household.

JACK BUSTEED: STRICT AND PARTICULAR METHODIST

No consideration of either Day Place or religion in Tralee can omit John 'Jack' Busteed, described by local histories as a 'strict and particular Methodist'.[5] The same histories describe him as taking over the *Kerry Evening Post* at some point in the late eighteenth century and establishing his printing works at no. 1 Day Place, where he was also the town's postmaster. But it is clear that there were in fact two John Busteeds, father and son. There were other members of the Busteed family in the Tralee area who have also been confused with both John Busteeds. Combined, the two 'Jack' Busteeds left much evidence of their activities, and religious and political beliefs, but it is necessary to unpick the two individuals to gain a clearer picture.

### JACK BUSTEED SENIOR

In July 1863 the death notice of the younger John Busteed states that the *Post* had been founded by his father eighty-nine years earlier.[6] A history of Co. Kerry written in 1871 said that 'Dr Busteed' came into Kerry in about 1780 and, 'as far as we can learn, bought up the proprietorship of the *Kerry Journal*, a still older paper'.[7] A 2005 book states baldly that the *Journal* had been started in 1772 and renamed as the *Kerry Evening Post* by Busteed on his acquiring the paper in 1775.[8] No copies of the *Kerry Journal* survive, and the earliest issue of the *Post* that still exists is dated 24 May 1813. It carries the inscription 'Vol. XXXVIII', and if a volume corresponds to a year then counting back thirty-eight years brings us to 1775.[9] Unfortunately, the 1813 issue is very much an outlier, the next surviving copy being dated 22 December 1824. The 1813 *Post* was printed at Tralee by John Busteed and Sons, proprietors. By 1824 the paper was printed by 'John Busteed, no. 1 Day Place'. We know that the proprietor in 1824 is the younger Jack Busteed as his father died in March 1819. His death was noted in the *Gentleman's Magazine* in the following terms: 'In Tralee, John Busteed esq., many years proprietor of *The Kerry Evening Post*'.[10]

*Postmaster and publisher*

Whether Jack Busteed senior had any connection with Day Place cannot be ascertained. He was the proprietor of a newspaper in Tralee before the terrace was begun. Like his son, he was postmaster. Mary O'Connell complains twice in her correspondence to Daniel O'Connell, in 1801 and 1802, that Mrs Busteed, the postmaster's wife, was believed to have read some of the mail from Dublin before giving it out to recipients.[11]

## JACK BUSTEED JUNIOR: POSTMASTER, PUBLISHER AND PROSELYTIZER

As he was 72 years old on his death in 1863, the younger Jack Busteed was born around 1791.[12] He had a short career as an officer in the 16th Regiment of Foot. In 1812 he was commissioned but was placed on half-pay in March 1817.[13]

In 1818 he was appointed postmaster of Tralee.[14] With his father's death in March of the following year he became proprietor of the *Kerry Evening Post*. Much of the income of the newspaper came from government contracts. In the second quarter of 1819 the paper had received payments totalling £41 7s. 1½d. for placing advertisements showing the average prices of corn and grain in the different ports of Ireland, a similar notice regarding sales in Dublin and its liberties, a proclamation forbidding the sale of gunpowder to ports in Africa and the West Indies and the revocation of a proclamation declaring that parts of Co. Louth were in a state of disturbance.[15]

Like his father, Busteed junior was a prominent 'dissenter'. By September 1819 his religious activities had brought him into conflict with the Established Church in the person of Edward Herbert, new curate of Tralee.[16] According to a piece published by Busteed, Herbert had been campaigning to close down the Sunday school operated by the Methodists and he accused him of having the 'zeal and hatred united of the most lynx-eyed bigotry'. Fearing the loss of government patronage, he wrote to the new chief secretary, Charles Grant.[17] He claimed that Herbert's supporters had been making efforts to damage his reputation within Co. Kerry, but public opinion had been on his side. He now felt that the conspirators had been at work in Dublin Castle and he was 'menaced through some unknown interference with the removal of that government patronage so long extended'.[18] The civil servants in Dublin discounted these suggestions, with one writing on top of the letter 'have efforts of this kind been made?' An official from the Gazette Office dismissed the allegations, instead explaining that Busteed had already received (or exceeded) the amount allowed.[19]

Busteed's religious activities also brought him into conflict with the Catholic church. He was the subject of strongly worded complaints from both Daniel O'Connell and Cornelius Egan, bishop of Kerry. Along with his brother Dr Morgan O'Connell Busteed, he worked with Revd McCrea to establish schools under the auspices of the London Hibernian Society. The society had been formed in London in January 1806 for 'The Diffusion of Religious Knowledge in Ireland'. It claimed to admit boys, girls and adults of every religious persuasion and was at pains to stress that no distinction was made 'of sect, party or denomination'. The only books provided were spelling books and New Testaments. The spelling lessons were entirely drawn from the scriptures.[20]

Although the schools claimed to be non-denominational, the Catholic establishment was convinced their purpose was conversion. Egan wrote in a letter in 1824:[21]

> John Busteed, the Tralee post-master ... a man tremblingly alive to the interests of Methodism, a constant intruder upon the poor confined in our county hospital, endeavouring to impress upon them the absurdities of the Popish and the reasonableness of the Methodistical tenets ... Morgan O'Connell Busteed MD, brother to the former, is no less zealous for the interests of Calvinism, than John for those of Methodism ... Were I to detail to you one half of the efforts made by the satellites to this *par nobile fratrum* to convert tradesmen, labourers and any other description of persons who may come within the sphere of their attention, my letters would swell to too great a bulk. These sir, with the Revd Mr McCrea are the principal agents employed in this neighbourhood by the London Hibernian Society and you will allow they are not the best guardians for Catholic children.

Egan went on to allege that a letter-carrier employed to bring mail to and from Listowel and Milltown had been threatened with dismissal if he did not send his children to one of the society's schools.[22]

In 1824 Busteed wrote to the Catholic Association offering a large sum of money towards circulating 40,000 copies of the Douai Bible with the condition that there would be no notes instructing the reader how to interpret the text. O'Connell was enraged, saying that 'Mr Busteed was a member of a society of fanatics at Tralee, the ladies of which are in the habit of bringing meat to the children of the schools patronised by the Society, on Fridays'.[23] In the following year Busteed chaired a meeting at Tralee Courthouse of Protestants of the county, which issued a petition declaring there was scriptural authority for 'complete and unshackled religious toleration, and free discussion of religious opinion'.[24] In 1826 Egan received a petition from 500 Catholics of the county of Kerry for 'permission to read the Bible'. O'Connell was again infuriated. He rejected the authenticity of the petition, saying that it was 'a thing got up by one Busteed, who keeps the Post Office in Tralee, and who uses the means that situation affords to circulate controversial tracts throughout the country', and went on to dismiss the signatories as 'a few small petty farmers and some persons connected with the Post Office', claiming 'it had not a single respectable signature attached to it'.[25] In 1827 a case came before the Tralee quarter sessions concerning the persecution of a Catholic who had converted to Protestantism. A Catholic magistrate made a statement that Busteed 'received £300 a year from the Missionaries for circulating whatever falsehoods they could collect'.[26]

Busteed's conduct as both postmaster and newspaper proprietor was under constant attack in the pages of the rival newspapers to the *Post*, the *Western Herald* and the *Tralee Mercury*, throughout the 1830s. The *Mercury* reported in February 1830 that its subscribers in outlying parts of the county were receiving their newspapers six to eight days late as a direct result of Busteed's mismanagement of deliveries.[27] In May of 1833 the *Western Herald* published an article entitled 'Post Office Plunder of Newspapers' in which they sarcastically pointed out the conflict of interest that 'this upright postmaster' might have.[28] In October 1833 the *Herald* published a story, 'Tralee Post Office – Reformed!!!', in which they claimed an official from Dublin had investigated and remedied a long list of abuses in Busteed's establishment, the most serious of which was the delaying and opening of mail from London.[29] The story was copied by the *Mercury*, who printed a retraction within days.[30] Busteed launched legal proceedings against both newspapers in the following year.[31] The attacks continued and in November 1835 a letter writer to the *Mercury* mocked 'Preacher Busteed' and the 'sundry odd-looking Christians' who wrote the 'dull, prolix, unintelligible articles' published in the *Post*. There were also allegations of corruption among the local constabulary who it was claimed were spying on the Catholic clergy at the direction of Busteed and his associates.[32] In 1836 a satirical play, *The Rueful Swaddler*, was written about the conduct of Protestants during the election of a member of parliament for Tralee in the previous year. Busteed was one of those parodied along with some of his neighbours at Day Place. The *Mercury* printed part of the play and was successfully sued for libel.[33]

In 1837 Busteed disposed of the *Kerry Evening Post* unceremoniously. The issue of 27 May bore his name at 1 Day Place while the following issue of 31 May had that of the new owners, John and Charles Eagar of The Mall.[34] In 1840 he resigned from his job as postmaster.[35] In 1842 he was still listed as a tenant at no. 1.[36] Early in the following year he refused to pay rates to the Tralee Town Commissioners, claiming that they were not carrying out their functions or keeping proper books of account.[37] On 1 February 1843 his goods were seized by the commissioners and sold to pay his debt.[38] Evicted from no. 1 Day Place, he was soon back in the terrace, living at no. 8 in 1846.[39] In February 1851 he married for a third time and moved to Dublin where he spent the rest of his life.[40] In 1855 he advertised no. 8 for rent, furnished, by the month or half year.[41]

P.D. JEFFERS AND DAVID MORIARTY: 'TAKING DAY PLACE BY STORM'

The most striking aspect of Day Place has been, since the 1870s, the Dominican Church of the Holy Cross, which closes off the view to the south (fig. 2). It overshadows the terrace while its neo-Gothic architecture contrasts with the classical proportions of the terrace of town houses. This odd juxtaposition, along with the cast-iron fence that separates Day Place from the through-traffic of the main road, creates an attractive urban space. It also illustrates, in three-dimensional form, a competition to dominate the terrace, and by extension the town, by competing religious groups. This varied from ill-tempered newspaper commentary to outright sectarianism and window-smashing.

The driving force and financial backer of Catholic revival was wealthy solicitor Patrick David Jeffers. This Tralee-born lawyer made his fortune in Dublin. During his life he funded the activities of Catholic education and evangelism. Following his death, a trust created by his will continued this work, while he found a final resting place in the sanctuary of Holy Cross. Jeffers worked hand-in-hand with Bishop David Moriarty, a figure of hate to certain Protestant parties.[42]

Jeffers's first connection with Day Place was in 1854. In that year the Sisters of Mercy arrived in Tralee. Two members of the order, accompanied by Bishop Moriarty, came to the town to organize the foundation of a convent there. The Sisters were rapidly expanding their activities throughout Ireland and a history of the order written in 1888 notes that 'they took possession of a suitable house in Day Place, which was rented for them by P. Jeffers Esq. and furnished by the townspeople'.[43]

The 'suitable house' was no. 1 Day Place. The sisters vacated the terrace in 1858, the site of a new convent having been donated on the edge of the town by the merchant John Mulchinock.[44] The house was recorded as being available to let in August 1858.[45] In 1860 the *Tralee Chronicle* announced it had moved its 'newspaper and general printing establishment' to no. 1, and would be publishing issues three times a week instead of twice.[46] The *Chronicle* was the town's Catholic rival to the Protestant *Kerry Evening Post* that Busteed had published in the same building until 1837.

ST MARY'S SEMINARY

A Catholic school, known as St Mary's Seminary, was established at no. 10 Day Place in 1855, operating 'under the patronage of the Right Revd David Moriarty and clergy'.[47] Prior to 1855 the occupants of no. 10 were firmly Protestant. The head of household was Mrs Deborah Day, widow of Revd Edward Day. Edward had been a first cousin once removed of Robert Day, the developer of Day Place.

A writer going under the *nom de plume* 'A.B.C.' wrote to the editor of the *Tralee Chronicle* about how he was struck by the appearance of the boys issuing from the house and was told that it was 'a school recently got up by the Roman Catholic coadjutor bishop'. Some of the boys had crosses on their caps and others did not. He had

been informed that the boys without crosses were the children of
Protestant gentlemen who had no good school of their own faith to
attend. He finished by lamenting that the local Protestants had been
unable to establish their own educational establishment.[48] This letter
may have been mischievous or an attempt to stir up sectarian feelings.
Its publication in the town's Catholic and Nationalist newspaper and
its characterization of the Protestant gentry suggest it may even have
been satire. At this remove it is hard to know but it received a rebuttal
a few days later. 'Verax', writing to the editor of the *Kerry Evening
Post*, sought to correct the record. As far as Protestant boys attending
the school and being specially marked out were concerned, he was
entirely dismissive. He stated that there was 'not one Protestant
pupil at the bishop's school, and from what I have heard, I believe a
Protestant could not consistently with his principles send his children
there'. 'Verax' went on to point out that any native of Tralee would
know that the removal of crosses from the caps was to show that
boys had broken the school rules and were thus publicly shamed.
He reminded readers that there was a Protestant school immediately
opposite Day Place which was 'attended by the sons of some of the
most respectable gentlemen about Tralee, who are being prepared for
the several universities, and for military and merchant professions'.
He ended by urging 'A.B.C.' not in his 'poetic ravings ... to draw
conclusions so derogatory to the Protestantism of Tralee'.[49]

   This peculiar exchange shows a tension between adherents of the
Catholic and Protestant creeds, albeit coded and filtered through the
letters pages. There can be absolutely no doubt of the attitude of 'One
From The West', however, who wrote to the editor of the *Post* from
Dingle in May 1855. As well as attacks on the character of Bishop
Moriarty, the writer drew parallels to the Crimean War, then at its
height. The letter writer found Moriarty's reintroduction of religious
orders to the town and patronage of Catholic schools alarming and
mentioned Day Place in particular:

> We hear of great doings going on among you in Tralee under
> Doctor Moriarty's generalship. He has, we are told, his seminary
> of holy boys, with crosses in front of their caps, drilling as
> regularly as the Militia – all to promote Christian charity and
> brotherly love of course. He is besieging Tralee right, left and

at all corners, with Sisters and Brothers of Mercy and piety. We are informed that he means to take Day Place by storm, and to convert the whole row by hook or by crook. – Sebastopol is not more closely invested. There's the Sisters of Mercy, like the French, have the left attack, and a housefull [*sic*] of Friars, like the English, have the right. Between them the Row must be in a safe position and a blessed state.

The school at no. 10 was described approvingly in the *Chronicle*, linking it to the fortunes of the merchant class and economy of Tralee: 'In this rising town, a sound commercial and mathematical education was a desideratum'.[50] It came to an end in 1861 with the arrival of the Dominicans and fresh controversy.

### THE DOMINICANS AND THE DAY PLACE GATE CONTROVERSY

In March 1861 the proprietor of the *Tralee Chronicle* advertised that he was letting much of no. 1 Day Place.[51] On 5 April Bishop Moriarty secured for the Dominicans the lease of no. 1, which they shared with the printing works of the *Chronicle* until 1863. They converted part of the house to a chapel and from February 1862 there was also a school on the site.[52] The Holy Cross Seminary held its first examinations in August 1862.[53] The small chapel in Day Place was not sufficient for their needs and an existing building across the main road at Godfrey Place was consecrated. A former slaughterhouse, it was named Holy Cross Church and on 4 August 1862 Mass was celebrated there to honour the feast day of their founder.[54]

In September 1862 Tralee became the site of religious riots. The Italian preacher, Alessandro Gavazzi, gave a virulently anti-Catholic lecture at the ballroom of Benner's Hotel. Several Catholics were violently ejected from the meeting and this led to a mob taking to the streets and smashing the windows of Protestant residences. Day Place was a target, although business premises throughout the town were attacked. Order was restored only when the Kerry Militia joined forces with the constabulary to clear the streets.[55]

The newly opened Dominican chapel and the house at no. 1 were either side of a fence that runs along the length of the terrace, forming a boundary between the paved area in front of the houses and the main road. In the febrile atmosphere following the riots, the fence became the cause of a dispute. In August 1863 there were allegations of underhand religious motives for the blocking of a gateway through the fence. To set the scene, it will be helpful to explain how the fence appeared and who put it there.

When Day Place was built, a branch of the Lee, known as the Big River, flowed past it, dividing it from Stoughton's Row and Godfrey Place. A wall was built, and trees planted by the riverbank. This was recalled by local historian Annie Rowan,[56] who grew up in the neighbouring Bridge House (later the constabulary barracks), in her column *Old Tralee and its Neighbourhood*: 'All along by Day Place there was a wall ... a green strip of grass and handsome row of trees at the river side'.[57] The first-edition Ordnance Survey town plan of Tralee of 1841 clearly shows this feature.[58]

By 1845 the 'town arch' or culverting of the Big River had been completed, and the Tralee Town Commissioners were turning their attention to lighting and improving this reclaimed area. In September they resolved to place lamps at Day Place and called for the removal of the 'unsightly wall'.[59] This led to an argument about whether the area was under their jurisdiction or private property as it was not a thoroughfare. The *Kerry Evening Post* of 20 September was full of correspondence on the matter. Major Fairfield of no. 2 Day Place (see ch. 3) published a long legal defence of the rights of private property while a letter writer going by the name 'Junius' put forward an argument that the grand jury of the county had long exercised rights there. There was also a letter claiming to come from 'The Big Tree in Day Place', invoking the spirits of past residents and complaining that although the 'weakest go to the wall' he would have no wall to go to.[60] The wall remained as arguments went to and fro until 1850. In that year the landlord of Day Place, Revd Edward FitzGerald Day, became chairman of the Town Commissioners. He took down the wall and replaced it with a cast-iron fence at his own expense, approvingly described as 'tasteful improvements' by the press.[61] Having explained the existence of this fence, we must return to 1863 and the allegations of sectarianism in a letter to the *Chronicle* written by the pseudonymous 'Catholic':

> Sir, – I should hope it is scarcely necessary to call your immediate attention to the bigoted act of intolerance which has been effected within the last few days in Day Place, by a certain Protestant clique who contributed funds for a gate which is placed in the centre of the railing opposite the Dominican church, thus shutting up a public passage which the Dominican Fathers and the Catholic congregation have a perfect right to use in approaching their place of worship. If I am not much mistaken as to their pluck and determination, the Catholics of Tralee will not submit to have their rights interfered with.[62]

On the following day the *Post* published an editorial in which they spluttered in reply: 'We have been pained by reading … a mischievous attempt to create religious ill-feeling in our town' they began. They condemned the 'intolerant and vicious-minded correspondent trying to do such mischief by a distortion of the truth'. They were disappointed that the *Chronicle* had published the letter and noted that if they had made some inquiries, they 'would not have libelled the Protestants of that, the most respectable locality in Tralee'. According to the 'facts' presented by the *Post*, Revd FitzGerald Day's tenants had complained some years earlier that the opening in the railing led to 'the commissioning of unseemly nuisances before their houses' and had asked that he close the gap. This referred to children crossing over from the Abbey area of town, which was a poor slum district, and congregating in Day Place. These conversations had gone on long prior to the arrival of the Dominicans at no. 1 or the fitting out of the chapel opposite. When the job was finally done, he substituted a gate for a railing, and provided a key for every resident 'including, of course, the Dominicans' (fig. 3). They finished their tirade by calling the claims that there was a public right of way as ridiculous and impertinent. 'The proprietor of the railing has as perfect a right to shut up this passage as he would have to close a window in his private dwelling-house'.[63]

The allegations and counter-allegations continued in the leaders of the two newspapers into September. The *Chronicle* said that the *Post*'s 'story about the Revd Mr FitzGerald Day is simply "a story"'. In their opinion, the gate had been erected quite deliberately to deter the Dominicans as 'an annoying, though very paltry, effort to embarrass

**3.** The controversial Day Place gate still in place in October 2022

them in the discharge of their sacred offices'. They went on to claim that the gate had been placed there by private subscription and that all the residents of the terrace had been asked to contribute with the exclusion of the Dominicans. In addition, they stated that 'neither Mr

Day, nor anyone else, has a right to close this passage'.[64] This brought
an angry reply from the *Post* in which their true colours appeared:[65]

> We are as much opposed to the religion of Rome in this land
> as is consistent with fair play and Christian charity; but we
> should be very sorry to fight the battles of Protestantism by
> such petty weapons as making a clergyman walk some dozen or
> twenty steps additional every day – which is the outside of the
> interference with the Dominicans in this case, even supposing
> the most distorted and exaggerated statements of the *Chronicle*
> to be true.

The *Chronicle* refused to withdraw 'one word' but said it would
no longer discuss this 'small, though unpleasant topic'.[66] The *Post*
made no such promise and defended the rights of the householders
of Day Place to the private enjoyment of the piece of land in front of
their residences while accusing the *Chronicle* of stirring up potential
sectarian violence:[67]

> The piece of gravelling and flagging within the railings referred
> to in the discussions, are the private property of Mr DAY, as an
> easement to the houses of Day Place, of which he is the landlord;
> and the public have no other right in them than, at the utmost,
> a right for a pedestrian to pass along in front of the houses, and
> out the lower end through a kind of turn stile … We all know
> what denunciations addressed to the excitable and prejudiced
> mob generally result in – broken windows, and it may be broken
> bones.

Revd FitzGerald Day arrived in Tralee on 9 September and
found himself involved in a controversy of which he had not been
forewarned. Resident in England, he had been travelling for ten days
and had not seen any of the hot-blooded leaders and letters that had
adorned the pages of the two newspapers. It was with evident dismay
that he wrote a letter to the editors of both journals from a Tralee
hotel. He set out his version of events: two years earlier, he had been
approached by his tenants at Day Place, who complained that

much annoyance was being incurred by means of the gap or ope in the centre of the railings which forms the boundary of that terrace at present, as troops of idle boys, attracted by its convenient position, continually flocked through it from opposite Day Place, which they made their daily rendezvous.[68]

The solution suggested, and to which he agreed, was to place a stone base and wrought-iron railing to seal the gap and match the existing fence. This work was to be done at the expense of the residents. Having been absent from Tralee, he was not aware that the work had not been completed at that time. In April 1863 he received communication from the Dominicans at no. 1, who informed him that the opening was about to be closed and that this was widely believed to be in order to obstruct them from reaching the chapel. This was causing 'considerable public excitement'. FitzGerald Day proposed that instead of permanently closing the gap, he would pay for the hanging of a door or gate and any resident who wished to have a key could do so. This the Dominicans agreed to and he duly ordered his smith to carry out the work. He vehemently denied that keys had been refused under any pretext to residents and also stated that no public rates had ever been spent, lighting, flagging or repairing Day Place and that the Town Commissioners had no rights over his private property. He ended by hoping that the unfounded allegations published in the *Chronicle* would 'with equal publicity, be fully and unreservedly retracted'.[69]

The *Chronicle* did no such thing and stated in a leader that they had nothing to retract and queried several points in FitzGerald Day's letter. This forced him into writing a second letter on 11 September in which he demanded a 'frank and manly retraction'.[70] The *Chronicle* dismissed the second letter in their edition of 15 September, mocking his 'feeble force'.[71]

The matter seems to have ended there. The *Post* of 19 September approved that the *Chronicle* had finally withdrawn from the controversy, but had not had, 'we regret to say, the grace to make the slightest *emende* to those … misrepresented and calumniated'.[72]

What are we to make of this incident? It seems that a newly made wrought-iron gate arrived at a difficult time in relations between two religious communities. The two rival newspaper editors appear to have purposely fed the fire with characterizations of a 'Protestant clique' on the one hand and 'the excitable and prejudiced mob' on the other. Clearly there were bigger issues being fought out than an argument over a right of way, and it would be interesting to see if this unpleasant episode had parallels in other parts of Ireland. In any case, the Protestants of Day Place were soon to suffer two major defeats at the hands of Patrick Jeffers.

### 'ONE OF THE MOST GLORIOUS CATHOLIC REVIVALS OF THE AGE': THE NEW HOLY CROSS CHURCH

In January 1865 a notice appeared in the *Tralee Chronicle* announcing that, following ten months of negotiations, the house and premises of William Denny had been purchased by the Dominican Fathers on Christmas Eve of the previous year.[73] William Denny was the younger brother of Edward Denny and was agent for the Denny estate. He was also a deputy lieutenant for Co. Kerry and had been a provost of the extinct corporation of Tralee (see ch. 3). Following the sale, he moved into no. 6 Day Place.[74] The property the Dominicans had acquired was described as 'a good house and extensive' with 'a good-sized yard and garden'.[75]

The order had to take out a loan of £2,000 to buy the house, of which £500 was repaid by P.D. Jeffers.[76] As Jeffers is to loom large for the rest of this chapter, it will help to provide some biographical details. Fortunately, he provided many of these himself when giving evidence to a select committee in July 1848.[77] By then a solicitor in Dublin, he had started his career in Kerry as assistant to Sir Matthew Barrington, crown solicitor on the Munster circuit, a post he held for thirteen years and after which he was sessional solicitor for Co. Kerry 'for five or six years'. He was proud to say that he had been brought 'into contact with the lower orders of people, probably to as great extent as anyone in Ireland, and I have had the means of knowing a good deal about their feelings and habit and condition'. He followed Barrington into private practice in Dublin, becoming a partner in the firm of Barrington, Son and Jeffers. In May 1835 he married Anna Fagan of Booterstown and seems to have left Tralee for good in 1836.[78]

Jeffers was a successful lawyer, specializing in the promotion of legislation to construct railways in Ireland. This involved him

Lapidem angularem Benedixit David
Moriarty Eps Kerriensis Festo Sæ Mæ Assæ AD
1866 inter rudera Cœnobii Sæ Crucis posuit
Anna (cujus reliquiæ conditæ sunt in hac
Ecclesia) uxor P.D.Jeffers Benefactoris insignis
Hiberniæ Prouls Adm. Reuo B.T.Russell
Conutus Priore Adm Reu.T.R.Rush Præfecto
rerum civilium Henrico J.Donovan

**4.** The cornerstone of Holy Cross Church laid in an elaborate ceremony in 1866

travelling to Westminster.[79] He remained devoted to his home town, and in 1840 wrote from Dublin offering to donate five pounds to the Tralee Temperance Society to help them provide a library for 'the intelligent and well-educated working men of Tralee' and offering to select some books he thought would be suitable.[80] When the long-anticipated bill to bring a railway to Tralee was in danger from Killarney-based objectors in 1853 he felt compelled to write to the *Chronicle* to defend the promoters.[81]

Returning to the 1860s, plans for the new church proceeded rapidly. In March 1866 the *Dublin Builder* gave some details: the architectural firm of Pugin and Ashlin had been employed and the project would cost £6,000. Building materials were to be imported from south-west England: rock-faced granite, Bath stone and Combe Down stone.[82]

In August 1866 work began in earnest. In a ceremony that was a celebration of Catholic resurgence and Nationalism, the cornerstone of the church was blessed by Bishop Moriarty and laid in place by Anna Jeffers, 'attended by her most excellent husband'. This she performed using 'a very beautiful trowel and mallet, the former of

solid silver, mounted in ivory, and the latter in Irish bog oak richly
wrought' (fig. 4).[83] There had previously been a Dominican priory in
the vicinity, which was destroyed in 1653 and it was implied that the
new church was a restoration of the extinct institution. The *Tralee
Chronicle* lost all perspective as it described it as a 'day memorable in
the history of Kerry, and long remembered in the annals of Catholic
Ireland. ... one of the most glorious Catholic revivals of the age'.
The previous Dominican church had, according to the *Chronicle*,
been 'razed to the ground by the ruthless hands of the sacrilegious
despoilers to whom poor Ireland was yielded up a bound and bleeding
victim in the days of the miscalled "Reformation"'. Indeed, Thaddeus
Moriarty, the last prior of the old Holy Cross, was said to be looking
down approvingly 'from his throne among the martyrs'.[84]

The prior gave a speech in which he praised Patrick Jeffers as
a 'princely donor' but also gave a clue to some of the setbacks and
alterations that had taken place. The walls were now to be of local
red sandstone rather than imported granite, while the proximity of
the site to the subterranean Big River had caused numerous problems
in building foundations. Only £5,200 of the £6,000 needed had been
raised, meaning that funds to build the upper portion of the tower
and the spire were still needed.[85] The stumpy tower remained waiting
for completion until 1958 when hopes were finally abandoned, and an
unimpressive roof was added.[86]

Anna Jeffers died in July of the following year at their Dublin
home. Interred in the family vault in St Mary's Church, Marlborough
Street (now the Pro-Cathedral), the officiating clergy included Dr
Rush, Dominican prior of Tralee.[87] A 'month's mind' was held in
August in the improvised Holy Cross chapel over the road from the
building site of the new church.[88]

The church was opened for services on 14 September 1871 and the
*Chronicle* gushed: 'Who that looks at Holy Cross Abbey and Church
can fail to feel his heart stirred within him to his deepest throb?',
they asked.[89] With much pride, they reported that 'it was ordained
that a Kerryman, the great O'CONNELL, should have been the
chosen instrument for the great consummation. He broke our fetters
and freed our Altars'. This followed two centuries of 'midnight,
of persecution, of bloodshed, of destruction'.[90] In equally flowery
language, they described how 'our great and good bishop beckoned

to the children of DOMINIC to return to their old home'.[91] Reports of the opening of the new church described its construction and features in some detail: Cork red marble and Galway green marble had been incorporated as a display of Irishness and the various donors and contractors were named and praised, Jeffers among them[92]

## 'GOOD CHRISTIANS, GOOD CITIZENS AND USEFUL MEMBERS OF SOCIETY': THE JEFFERS INSTITUTE

Shortly before the opening of Holy Cross Church on 22 July 1871 Jeffers made a will leaving the bulk of his estate for the foundation of a school for Catholic boys from the labouring and working classes of Tralee to enable them to enter university and the professions.[93]

Jeffers died suddenly aged 62 in London on 30 April 1873. He had been in the British capital to ensure the passage of the Dublin Tramways Bill when he collapsed and died shortly afterwards from a heart condition.[94] His remains arrived at Tralee station on the evening of 5 May accompanied by members of the Dominican order, his legal colleagues and directors of the Great Southern and Western Railway Company.[95] His body was carried by hearse in a massive oak coffin to Holy Cross Church and he was placed in a vault the next day following requiem Mass.[96] This was in accord with the first part of his will:

> I desire that I shall be buried in the chapel of the Dominican convent in the town of Tralee and I desire that the remains of my beloved mother and my beloved wife Anna shall be removed from my vault in the Catholic Church, Marlborough Street, and laid with mine in the same vault in the chapel of the Dominican convent, Tralee.[97]

Having provided sums for such purposes as the receiving of 'fallen women' by the Sisters of Mercy, he left the residue:

> to found and maintain a perpetual charity the object of which shall be to give a good education to boys native of Tralee or its immediate neighbourhood, children of the working and labouring classes and not of gentlemen or of persons belonging

to a higher class whose talents and qualities may afford
reasonable hopes of their rising in life if they are well educated
... to forward them in life in college, professions, mercantile,
agricultural, scientific or commercial pursuits so that by the
blessing of God the foundation I desire may be a perpetual
means of enabling poor youths of Tralee and its neighbourhood
to rise from poverty and obscurity to positions of wealth, utility
and distinction thus securing good Christians, good citizens and
useful members of society who may do credit to their county
and benefit their fellow men.[98]

The school that Jeffers wished to create as his legacy took more
than thirty years to open. When it did, it was at no. 1 Day Place,
at the opposite end of the terrace to his final resting place. Events
had overtaken the trustees of the will, as a form of secondary or
'intermediate' education had been introduced by statute in 1878.[99]
In the following year there was a major reorganization of what we
would now call third-level education, with the creation of the Royal
University of Ireland.[100] This resulted in a demand for schools to
prepare students for examinations to enter university. John Coffey,
Catholic bishop of Kerry, established the Intermediate and University
School in Denny Street, Tralee, staffed by members of diocesan
clergy. At the same time the (Protestant) Intermediate School was set
up in Nelson Street.[101]

In 1897 the lease of no. 1 Day Place became available and was
taken by Bishop Coffey, and the Intermediate and University School
moved to the building.[102] At the 1901 census the school had eighteen
rooms with two resident priests and a domestic servant.[103] In April
1904 Bishop Coffey died and the trustees of Jeffers's will bought the
lease from his estate for £500.[104] The Patrick David Jeffers Charity
was formed and in 1906 the Jeffers Institute came into existence.[105]
Father Jeremiah Buckley, who had been principal of the defunct
Intermediate and University School, took up the same position in the
institute. In other ways, the school was very different. Transformed
from a place where middle-class Catholics sent their sons to prepare
for university, the institute was a working-class school. In accordance
with the will and the charity's scheme of management, pupils had
to be 'sons of labourers and artisans in receipt of daily or monthly

wages or tradesmen or farmers occupying houses of less annual poor-law value than £7. Boys had to have been born within ten miles of Tralee and to have received a primary education and have Catholic parents. The primary purpose of the school was to ensure instruction in the Catholic faith. Its secondary purposes were instruction in English literature and composition, oratory and elocution, English and Irish history and 'modern history generally', modern geography, mathematics, 'pure and natural philosophy' and bookkeeping. If funds permitted, teaching in drawing, applied mechanics, building-trade subjects, shorthand, typewriting, chemistry and art was permitted. Jeffers had a low regard for foreign languages and a contempt for classical education. Accordingly, only if the preceding subjects had been 'thoroughly learnt' were students to be taught French and German and 'last of all, … Latin and Greek'.[106] It is striking that there was no mention whatsoever of the Irish language or music: a practical curriculum, not a 'Celtic revival' one.

### CONCLUSION

In some ways, 'One From The West', who wrote in such alarmed terms to the *Kerry Evening Post* in 1855, had been proved correct. By the time of the 1911 census the 'whole row' had been almost completely converted to Catholic occupation. The Jeffers Institute at one end and the Church of the Holy Cross at the other clearly indicated the triumph of the Catholic church. By December of that year the last remaining household of the now disestablished Church of Ireland fell with the death of James Coyle.[107]

The Catholic victory, however, was not so substantial. The Jeffers Institute struggled to find students as it competed with the new schools of the Tralee Technical Instruction Committee. In 1928 it vacated Day Place for shared premises in the former Fever Hospital in the Moyderwell area of Tralee.[108] No. 1 reverted to being a private residence. Patrick Jeffers's legacy lives on in the cornerstone of the Holy Cross Church, a building never completed, and in a scholarship trust created after the institute that bore his name was closed and demolished.[109] Its site is now occupied by a library, but there are few traces of him in the Local Studies Department housed there.

# 3. From 'Tory power' to the 'friends of the people'

The period under review was one of great reform in Irish local government. Changes in the 1830s and 1840s dismantled the arcane structures of both town and county administration, which had been assembled to favour the interests of landlords with little or no input from those who were forced to pay for it.[1] The legislation was created by the Westminster parliament in the interests of the United Kingdom. It mirrored reforms already carried out in Great Britain with variations specific to Irish conditions. There were two levels of administration: county and town. The county had been created for the administration of the law and had various functions thrown upon it which were not always efficiently carried out. Piecemeal reforms had limited impact until the introduction of Kerry County Council at the end of the nineteenth century. Tralee itself was a 'pocket borough' under the control of a self-selecting corporation created to ensure the election of members of parliament favourable to the Protestant cause. A town commission replaced it and began the work of managing and improving Tralee. Elections were often held on issues unconnected to its mundane duties and it became a test of the relative strength of Unionists and supporters of Home Rule. Additionally, there was the *ad hoc* administration of the poor law under a board of guardians, an amalgam of popularly elected members and *ex-officio* magistrates, and the harbour board, which had been formed by local act (see ch. 1).

## COUNTY GOVERNMENT

### High sheriff

The office of sheriff was theoretically the senior one in the county, providing a link between the vice-regal court at Dublin Castle and

Kerry. It was of great antiquity, dating from when the process of 'shiring' Ireland was carried out in the later Middle Ages. The once-impressive range of powers possessed by the high sheriff had slowly been reduced and by 1835 the main responsibilities were:[2]

- acting as returning officer for the elections of members of parliament for the county
- choosing the grand jury (see below)
- convening county meetings when petitioned to do so.

The sheriff's term of office was one year. The qualifications for nomination were very few. Those nominated were expected to reside in the county and by 1835 Catholics were permitted to hold the office. It was difficult to find potential candidates. The sheriff was required to provide a 'recognizance' of £1,000 to the crown and pay the salaries for sub-sheriffs and bailiffs. As the senior legal officer in the county, it was the sheriff's responsibility to ensure writs were served. This could involve evictions and the imprisonment of debtors. If a debtor escaped custody the sheriff could be sued by his creditor.[3]

## County lieutenancy and deputy lieutenants

Until 1831 the counties of Ireland had two officers: the governor, who awarded commissions in the militia, and the *custos rotulorum* (keeper of the rolls) who, inter alia, recommended suitable persons to be justices of the peace. In Great Britain these two offices were held by a single person known as 'his (or her) majesty's lieutenant of the county' and informally as lord lieutenant. In an Irish context this can be confusing as the viceroy in Dublin was known as the lord lieutenant of Ireland. County lieutenants were often peers of the realm and this was true in Kerry. Of the four lieutenants appointed from 1831 until the abolition of the lieutenancy on independence, three were viscounts of Kenmare. The remaining lieutenant was one of the Herbert family of Muckross, member of parliament for Kerry and briefly chief secretary of Ireland. Although Tralee was the county's most important and most industrialized town, it had no nobility. This was noted sourly by a special correspondent to the *Cork Daily Southern Reporter* in 1869: 'Nobles and princes and notables, who are plenty as blackberries in Killarney, are rare as white elephants in Tralee'.[4]

The 1831 legislation provided for the appointment of deputy lieutenants, 'proper and discreet persons', who were required to be living within or in an adjoining county and to possess property to the value of £200 or be the heir apparent to an estate of £400.[5] It also required connections, as names for deputy lieutenants had to be forwarded by the county lieutenant to the lord lieutenant of Ireland for approval. The number was limited, with the viceroy deciding on the number allocated to each county. Deputy lieutenants were appointed for life and could be removed only by the crown. Two of Day Place's residents were sufficiently wealthy and well-connected to acquire the coveted 'DL' suffix to their name.

## The grand jury

A curiosity of Irish local government was that most of the expenditure on county matters was authorized by the grand jury. As the name suggests, the grand jury's origins were as part of the legal system, and they decided if there was sufficient evidence to send cases on to the county assizes, which were held twice a year – the lent and summer assizes. Only the most serious of matters, such as murder, were dealt with at assizes.

The grand jurors were selected by the sheriff, who had total freedom of choice. It was expected that jurors be substantial landowners. The system was routinely misused, with sheriffs appointing friends and relatives. This was offset by the strict order of precedence and those appointed earlier remained at the top of the list, sometimes for decades. Only the most senior jurors who attended the assizes were empanelled, and newly added jurors had no guarantee they would ever join the panel.[6]

The grand jury was obliged to employ several officers under 1823 legislation. The annual salaries paid to the personnel in charge of the judicial functions for the county ranged from £350 for the clerks of the crown and peace to £12 for the judges' criers.[7] Perhaps the most important officer was the county treasurer. Also paid £350 a year, he had to prove he had property of £7,000, or twenty years income, and was not permitted payment from any other source.[8]

The grand jury met for presentments sessions immediately prior to the assizes. Presentments were requests for funds for public works drawn up by two persons in front of a justice of the peace. Most of the expenditure looked for was for the construction or repair of roads and bridges. The expected costs were given in the presentment, but this was not supported by quotations or evidence. With the lack of proper mapping, two or three presentments could be made for the same stretch of road and there was little monitoring of the quality of the work carried out. If approved, the cost was levied on the occupiers of land as the county cess (for 'county at large' purposes such as courthouses or gaols) or the baronial cess (paid by cess payers within a single barony, or sub-division of the county).

Unsurprisingly, the system was abused. As the cess was paid by the occupants and not the owners of land, it was possible for landlords to propose improvements paid for by their tenants. From 1834 there was a dramatic improvement as a qualified county surveyor was appointed in every county.[9] Contracts were now to be by sealed tender and a number of cess payers were to join the magistrates in the roads presentment sessions.[10] Some residents of Day Place managed to reach the heights of the grand jury, and some were among its senior employees.

*County Council*

By the 1890s the grand jury's role in Irish county government was out of step with the rest of the United Kingdom. Elected county councils had been created in England and Wales in 1889 and in Scotland in 1890, taking over duties from magistrates. 1898 legislation brought county councils to Ireland. Their constitution differed from their British counterparts, being mostly directly elected but also including the chairmen of the new rural district councils *ex officio* and a handful of co-opted members. The first election of county councillors was held on 6 April 1899. Of the twenty councillors elected across the county, only three were members of the outgoing grand jury.[11] On 8 April three members of the old grand jury were co-opted onto the new council.[12] The completed county council's membership of thirty contained twenty-four councillors completely new to county administration.

The county councillor elected for Tralee was a publican. His supporters paraded around the town with flaming torches and tar barrels and he wore a green sash given to him by the artisans and labourers of Tralee. It was not a complete change of the guard. A speech of celebration was given by Richard Latchford, former resident of Day Place, who was co-opted to the council a few days later.[13]

*The borough of Tralee*

In 1613 the 'village of Traly' was incorporated as a borough. The principal purpose of the incorporation was to create a parliamentary constituency that would send two members to the Dublin parliament loyal to King James I. No parliament had sat since 1586 and Tralee was one of forty new boroughs issued charters between December 1612 and May 1613.[14] The small and select corporation created by charter was the entire electorate. The fact that they were the first form of urban authority for Tralee was a necessary side effect.[15] The corporation created by the charter continued to operate until 1840 and the entry for Tralee in Lewis's *Topographical dictionary* of 1837 gives its formal structure, while a parliamentary report of 1833 shows how it worked in practice.[16]

The corporation was named the 'Provost, Free Burgesses and Commonalty of the Borough of Tralee' and consisted of a provost and twelve burgesses. The corporation was self-selecting and burgesses held office for life. In 1833 an inquiry was held in Tralee into the state of the corporation. The only advantages the commissioners could find for the town's occupants was that the provost held a court for the recovery of small debts and that two serjeants-at-mace acted as constables. The corporation had no property, and only a small stream of income from market tolls it shared with the Denny family and fees paid by its members on being elected as a free burgess or provost. It did not have the finances to carry out even its limited functions efficiently. The report concluded by saying that a 'feeling of dissatisfaction prevails among a large proportion of the inhabitants as to its close and practically exclusive character' and that the corporation was 'entirely unconnected with the trading and commercial classes, and the great body of the community are debarred from all interest or participation in its proceedings'.[17]

Municipal corporations in England and Wales were reformed by parliament in 1835 and legislation followed for Ireland in 1840. In

Britain, the majority of boroughs had retained their corporations, which were given a uniform structure and a council elected by ratepayers. In Ireland, only ten borough corporations survived in the largest towns and cities. The Municipal Corporations (Ireland) Act dissolved the remaining fifty-eight corporations. The date set for the extinction of Tralee Corporation was 25 October 1840. Section 25 of the act allowed for the ratepayers of an extinguished borough to choose to adopt the Lighting of Towns (Ireland) Act 1828 and elect Town Commissioners.

## Tralee Town Commissioners

One of the final official acts by the last provost of Tralee was to call a public meeting at Tralee Courthouse on 16 October. The 1828 act was adopted with much excitement as the five-pound householders were enfranchised for the first time and expected to 'behold the final dissolution of Tory power and influence' to be replaced by the 'well-known friends of the people'.[18] William Denny and Daniel Supple were identified as leaders of two 'parties' who had prepared lists of candidates. Reading between the lines, they were Unionist and Repeal lists. The meeting was adjourned until the following day when Denny withdrew his original list and presented twenty-one names for the twenty-one seats that had been agreed by both sides, and the need for an election was avoided. The names were published in a notice signed by the provost, which noted that the Tralee Town Commissioners would hold their first meeting on 24 October.

The Town Commissioners, unlike the borough corporation, had genuine powers to create improvements. As we have seen, they clashed with Day Place residents over the wall, a problem only resolved when the terrace's landlord replaced it with railings in 1850. John Busteed's refusal to pay rates was enough to have his goods seized in 1843 (see ch. 2).

The major innovation brought to Tralee by the commissioners was the lighting of the town by gas. The lamps installed can be seen on the earliest photographs of Day Place. In 1874 the commissioners were given new responsibilities as a sanitary authority.[19] The triennial elections were an opportunity for Nationalists to gain a foothold in local administration, especially from 1880 when almost all restrictions on eligibility for candidature were removed.[20]

*Urban district council*

The same act that brought Kerry County Council into existence imported another form of local government: the district council. As a larger town with sanitary powers, Tralee became an urban district. The first election of district councillors was held on 23 January 1899.[21]

*Tralee Board of Guardians*

The introduction of the English poor-law system and the creation of the Tralee Board of Guardians in 1840 added another level of administration to the area. The majority of the board was popularly elected, giving Nationalists a new opportunity. One quarter of the seats were reserved for local magistrates who were entitled to appoint members *ex officio*.

In January 1840, a meeting was held at Tralee Courthouse. An assistant poor-law commissioner from Dublin explained the new system. The board was to consist of forty-five guardians: thirty-four elected by and from the ratepayers and eleven appointed from among the magistracy.[22]

Elections for the first board of guardians for the Tralee Poor Law Union were held in April 1840. Surprisingly, the 'aristocratic' and 'popular' parties made efforts to avoid any elections and divided up the seats between themselves.[23] This was not to last, and guardian elections were to be a place where struggles between Unionist and Home Ruler and later Parnellite and Anti-Parnellite were bitterly played out.

### DAY PLACE AND LOCAL GOVERNMENT

Many of the Day Place householders were active in local government. The examples below include members of an ancient Gaelic family, an army officer and improving landlord, a public servant of dubious character and a doctor at the heart of Nationalist politics.

*Daniel McGillycuddy and descendants*

Daniel McGillycuddy was the fourth son of Cornelius McGillycuddy, the McGillycuddy of the Reeks, and his wife, Catherine Chute. The McGillycuddys had held onto a reputedly ancient Gaelic title while converting to the Established Church. The Chutes were a planter family with land to the east of Tralee. Born in 1755 in Tralee, Daniel married Sophia Denny, daughter of Sir Barry Denny, 2nd baronet, in Tralee parish church in 1811, cementing his place in the highest echelon of the Tralee establishment. He became agent to the McGillycuddy estate and was the first occupant of no. 4 Day Place.

A report to parliament in 1826 indicated that Daniel was appointed sub-sheriff of Co. Kerry in 1804. Four of his brothers were to hold the same office over the next eight years before Daniel himself became high sheriff in 1813.[24] Although his death is not recorded in the fragmentary remains of the local newspapers or parish registers of that time, we find his widow disposing of the leases of some property in the town in her own name in July 1830.[25]

McGillycuddys continued to live at no. 4 Day Place until 1901 as it was occupied successively by Daniel's son and grandson, Daniel de Courcy McGillycuddy senior and junior. Both were solicitors and agents to the McGillycuddy estate. Both were poor-law guardians and Town Commissioners. The death of the elder in 1882 was by suicide, apparently due to the workload involved in compensating tenants under the land acts.[26] The younger became sessional crown solicitor for Kerry, conducting prosecutions on behalf of the state.[27] By now comfortably part of the small and wealthy Protestant elite of Tralee, they were buried in an expensive plot in the most fashionable section of the town's New Cemetery.[28] Daniel de Courcy McGillycuddy junior was a leading member of the laity of the Church of Ireland, as his impressive memorial tablet in St John's Church tells us.

### Charles George Fairfield

According to his funereal monument, Charles George Fairfield was born in December 1799. He had an Indian-born English father and an Irish mother and was most likely born in India himself.[29] His family maintained connections with the East India Company until its demise. He obtained an ensigncy in the 3rd Foot Guards in July 1815. A prestigious regiment, the purchase of the commission would have involved a considerable financial outlay. The Napoleonic Wars had just ended, and Fairfield's military career was apparently uneventful. By 1822 Fairfield was on half-pay and in 1825 his finances may have been under strain as he disposed of his commission in the guards for a cheaper one in the 54th Regiment of Foot.

In 1829 he married Frances 'Fanny' Crosbie in London. She was one of two daughters and co-heirs of the late William Arthur Crosbie, member of the Irish parliament, who held part of the seigniory of Castleisland. Fairfield thus became the owner of an estate in Co. Kerry. William Crosbie's other co-heir married Berkeley Drummond three years later. Drummond was a career soldier and had spent thirty years in the 3rd Foot Guards.

Unlike Drummond, Fairfield was not an absentee landlord and quickly moved to Ireland. In 1830 he resigned from the army and in August was sworn onto the grand jury for Co. Kerry.[30] His wife remained in England. An invalid, she was at the health resort of Brighton in Sussex when she died later that year.[31]

Fairfield worked enthusiastically to improve his lands and, through a programme of road building via county presentments, opened up the area around the present village of Brosna.[32] He enjoyed a sporting life, building 'Mount Eagle Lodge' to house shooting parties.[33] A sycophantic contemporary described him as a 'brilliantly gifted and most attractive-looking officer of the guards' and 'a miracle worker in making the wilderness an oasis'.[34]

Fairfield was living at no. 2 Day Place by the spring of 1831. Already included in the county's commission of the peace, he was one of the first to hold a commission as a deputy lieutenant of Co. Kerry.[35] In July 1831 he was appointed a captain in the Kenmare Yeomanry and a major in the Kerry Militia in June 1849.[36] As Captain or Major Fairfield, he appears among the membership of numerous local bodies of which we shall explore only a handful.

In November 1832 he was named in the *Dublin Gazette* as high sheriff of Kerry for the ensuing year.[37] One of his first duties was to act as returning officer for the election of two members of parliament for the county in the first parliamentary contest following the passing of the Great Reform Act.[38] On Christmas Eve 1832 he attended at Tralee Courthouse where there were just two nominations for the two seats, both members of Daniel O'Connell's Repeal Association. Fairfield therefore declared the nominees elected without a poll.[39]

In his role as a deputy lieutenant he found himself asked to investigate unrest among the tenantry of the Dingle Peninsula and to inquire into faction fighting at Ballybunnion.[40] He may have made enemies as 'in the dead hour of the night' in February 1835 'ruffians' stole the rapper from the door of no. 2.[41]

When the first board of poor-law guardians was formed in 1840, Fairfield was one of the magistrates chosen to be a member.[42] He declined a nomination to be vice-chairman in 1841 as he felt he could not attend regularly enough.[43] A Tralee relief committee was formed in April 1846 to address the severe conditions in the town consisting of prominent merchants and gentlemen and clergy of all denominations. Fairfield was a very active member of the committee, which was chaired by William Denny and included Daniel de Courcy McGillycuddy and George Hilliard of nos 4 and 9 Day Place respectively.[44] He was described as 'emphatically the poor man's friend' who 'gave up his whole time, and devoted his great practical ability to the interests of the starving masses in our district'. His obituary in the *Kerry Evening Post* probably exaggerated the feelings of the working classes of Tralee: 'many a blessing have we heard heaped upon him then, and many an honest tear have we seen this day shed to his memory'.[45]

Fairfield's respectable position led to him being chosen to participate in the running of two private enterprises, which were expected to bring great prosperity to Tralee, but spectacularly collapsed in the 1840s, shortly before he left the town. The Tralee Savings Bank was established in 1823. It was part of a movement that had started in Britain, encouraging the poorer classes to lodge small amounts under the watchful eyes of trustees drawn from the landed, clerical and professional classes.[46] In the year he was high sheriff, 1833, Fairfield was chairman of the bank. He continued as a trustee for the remainder of its life.[47] In February 1844 he 'paid a most flattering and deserved compliment to John Lynch Esq., the secretary of the institution, for the zeal and efficiency with which he has discharged the duties of his office almost gratuitously'.[48] Four years later it emerged that Lynch, who ran the bank from his house, had embezzled about £28,000 over twenty years.[49] The Tralee bank was the first of three in Ireland that failed within weeks of each other, leading to permanent damage to the movement.[50] Lynch received the severe sentence of transportation for fourteen years while investors had to wait until 1877 to receive 2s. 6d. in the pound – 1.25 per cent of their deposits.[51]

By the 1840s railway mania had reached Tralee. The Great Munster Railway Company was formed in February 1845 with many of the leading gentry of Kerry on its provisional committee, including Fairfield.[52] The public were urged to rally around these men who had 'originated this great undertaking and given the influence of their high names, and devoted their time and money'.[53] Fairfield was appointed Irish general manager of the company. The *Kerry Examiner* had no doubt he was the right man for the job. 'Kerry may well feel flattered at the signal honour ... paid them in the appointment of Mr Fairfield to represent so respectable a body as that which constitutes the Great Munster Railway Company'.[54]

The respectability of the Great Munster was not deserved. Multiple railway companies were being floated and more failed than succeeded. In the 1845–6 parliamentary session alone 576 railway bills were introduced with a capital of over £300,000,000 being sought from investors.[55] The bill was withdrawn by the company in May 1846 and shareholders initiated an action to pursue the directors individually for loss, later settling out of court.[56]

The *Tralee Chronicle* of 1 December 1849 reported that Major Fairfield and family had left for his new residence in Dublin. He had become the agent for the Irish estates of the Hon. Sidney Herbert, younger brother of the earl of Pembroke and a member of the House of Commons.[57] In 1852 a decision was made to hold a 'Great Industrial Exhibition' in Dublin, following the example of the Great Exhibition of 1851 in London. Fairfield was appointed deputy chairman.[58] He attended the official opening in May 1853 when it was noted he had just recovered from a severe illness.[59] His recovery was temporary and he died on 16 October, 'breathing his last at half past six'.[60] It was reported that 'up to the period when his declining health prevented him, [he] exerted himself with untiring energy in promoting the success of this great undertaking'.[61] The Kerry newspapers recalled his role in the county: 'so much respected in every capacity, as grand juror, magistrate, poor-law guardian and who in social life was the idol of the circle in which he moved'.[62] His lands in Kerry reverted to his brother-in-law, and his 'wife and ... large interesting family' that survived him severed connections to the county.[63] His widow was living in England by 1855, and his surviving children were to be found in various parts of England, Australia and India in later years.[64]

*Charles Edward Leahy*

Richard Latchford's 'right, title and interest' in no. 6 Day Place were sold at auction in 1880.[65] The purchaser was Charles Edward Leahy. Not a great deal can be learnt about Leahy's early life apart from the fact he was from a Protestant Tralee family. His baptism is recorded in the register of St John the Evangelist's Church on 25 June 1856.[66] Exactly two months after purchasing no. 6 (25 January 1881), he married his next-door neighbour, Isabella Maria Quill, daughter of Jerome Quill JP of no. 7. Leahy was described as a merchant in the parish register.[67]

Although Leahy described himself variously as a merchant and a gentleman, he had taken the post of cess collector for the baronies of Iraghticonnor and Magonihy soon after arriving in Day Place.[68] The local-government board auditor's report of the grand-jury accounts of July 1884 mentioned him by name as 'persistently acting as if in total disregard' to the law. Collectors were required to regularly deposit monies and never to have more than £100 in their hands. Leahy had deposited nearly £10,000 just before the deadline of the spring assizes.[69] This strong rebuke seems to have had no effect, and in September 1887 he was appointed as receiver and rates collector by the Killarney Town Commissioners.[70] In 1888 he was added to the membership of the Fenit Pier and Harbour Commissioners.[71]

Although he continued as baronial-cess collector well into the 1890s, Leahy was also an entrepreneur. He became the owner of the Flesk Mills outside Killarney. In January 1890 he seems to have surprised the Killarney Town Commissioners by informing them that he was applying under the Electric Lighting Act to light the town using power generated by the water wheels at his mill.[72] The town was already partially lighted by gas and there was much correspondence and threats of legal action.[73] The conflict of interest of the town's rate collector providing services to the commissioners was skirted around. In May 1893 the first electric lamp post in Killarney was turned on in a public ceremony. Leahy was now chairman of the Killarney Electric Lighting Company.[74]

In October 1894 Leahy decided to dispose of no. 6, which he had been renting to the Barrett family (see ch. 1) for some years while living elsewhere.[75] In the following year the Barretts purchased the lease, becoming direct tenants of the Day family.[76]

Leahy's dubious behaviour continued. In January 1896 he was elected secretary of the harbour commissioners by the unimpressive margin of three votes to two with four abstentions.[77] Nine years later the commissioners found themselves embroiled in a scandal when they voted to increase Leahy's salary.[78] The chairman of the board objected and made his views known in the press. The *Kerry People*, a newly founded newspaper that portrayed itself as the voice of the ordinary public, was outraged. In an article entitled 'THAT DIRTY JOB', they claimed that 'no more flagrant effort to flout public opinion has ever been made, even in the history of jobbery in Kerry'. They compared the decision to the worst actions of the grand jury and argued that there was 'not the shadow of a shade of justification' for the pay raise.[79]

In a case of history repeating itself, an auditor's report was extremely critical of Leahy, but this time directly accused him of committing embezzlement. On the morning of 15 May 1906, the board met with Leahy present as secretary. A copy of the report was given to each board member to read and the meeting was adjourned until two in the afternoon. The auditor had 'discovered serious irregularities on the part of the secretary, which, in our opinion, are nothing short of misappropriation of the monies belonging to the commissioners and falsification of the books'. When the adjourned meeting resumed, Leahy was gone, having written a letter of resignation. In it he stated that the holding over of sums could have been 'very satisfactorily accounted for' but he had been busy. Unfortunately for the board, he had no time to fully explain as he had left for London.[80]

In the 1911 census of England he was living at his sister's house in the London suburbs.[81] He spent the rest of his life in that area, dying in November 1943.[82] His passing does not seem to have been recorded in any Irish newspaper. Leahy was able to take advantage of the weaknesses in local governance to advance himself socially and give himself a privileged lifestyle. Unfortunately for him, he did not have the finances to pay for it. Unfortunately for the ratepayers, he was entrusted with public funds. While he was not the only resident of Day Place to live well beyond his means, he was unique in diverting so much public money to make up the shortfall.

## John Mary Harrington

The *Freeman's Journal* of 24 June 1882 advertised the auction of Captain Richard Elliott Palmer's properties around Tralee (see ch. 1). Lot 5 was 'The valuable interest in the first-class residence, no. 2 Day place'.[83]

The purchaser was 'John M. Harrington MD'.[84] John Mary Harrington was a member of a new Catholic professional class, able to take advantage of the opening up of universities to members of his religion and funded by his entrepreneurial family. His father was Maurice Harrington, proprietor of the 'Monster House': a grocery and wine-and-spirit warehouse on the Lower Mall.

The *Medical directory* of 1883 gives details of his medical training. He had studied in Dublin at the Catholic University and Trinity College, graduating with a BA in 1877. In 1882 he received qualifications as a physician, surgeon and midwife, completing his training at the Rotunda and Dr Steeven's hospitals immediately prior to arriving in Tralee.[85]

He quickly began to play a prominent part in the life of the town. In 1885 he was listed as donating £2 to the building fund of Holy Cross Church and in the same year was one of the founding members of the Tralee Catholic Literary Society. The new organization was without premises and Harrington gave a fundraising lecture on 'The Irish Brigade in America'.[86] In the following year it was decided to form a branch of the Young Ireland Society in Tralee. Harrington addressed a public meeting where he said the people of the town needed to 'pay a tribute of respect to the men who were willing and ready to sacrifice everything in the sacred cause of Ireland and liberty'. The Michael Davitt branch of the society was formed with Harrington as president.[87]

Unsurprisingly, Harrington became a Town Commissioner in 1892 and in 1893 chairman of the Town Commission.[88] As chairman he was presiding officer at the next year's election of commissioners. Nationalists had split into 'Parnellite' and 'McCarthyite' factions and each side put up a full slate for the seven seats available. The Parnellites won five seats to the McCarthyites two, among them Michael B. Stokes of no. 5 Day Place (see ch. 1).[89] In 1895 Harrington was among the seven candidates nominated by the Tralee National Federation, an anti-Parnellite grouping. The Parnellites countered

**5.** No. 9 Day Place, proudly displaying the inscription 'T.C.L.S.' in September 2018

by nominating seven candidates including two Conservatives. It was a bitterly fought campaign and the Parnellites took five seats. Harrington found himself twelfth out of fourteen candidates, ending his membership of the body.[90]

In 1900 Harrington was instrumental in the Tralee Catholic Literary Society obtaining possession of no. 9 Day Place. In doing so, he literally left a mark on the town as the letters 'T.C.L.S.' still stand out proud between the first and second floors (fig. 5). In 1901 the first meeting of the society in its new premises was held with Harrington as chairman.[91] A plan for a gymnasium was discussed while a series of lectures and debates for the next month was agreed. The purchase of a billiard table was authorized and it was reported that the society's cycle club was fully organized with a programme of weekend outings already undertaken.[92] Although the TCLS flourished for six decades, it had a severe critic in D.P. Moran, who dismissed it for not being what he saw as culturally Irish: 'talk without action, and green nationality taking the place of sound Irish ideas'.[93]

Harrington's brand of Nationalism was being left behind. In October 1915 he was part of a group that welcomed John Redmond to the town to re-establish a branch of the United Ireland League in Kerry.[94] The UIL was a doomed Home Rule organization that supported Redmond's Irish Parliamentary Party, both of which were completely eclipsed by Sinn Féin.

Harrington continued to operate his medical practice and live at Day Place after independence, but he disappeared from local government. He died in the house in May 1931, aged 78. His widow followed one of his sons to Australia, where she died fifteen years later.[95]

Harrington was an example of a man who was to join the professions due to the 'new money' of the Catholic merchant class. He represented mainstream and moderate Irish Nationalism and cultural revival and for about two-and-a-half decades was an influential figure. His passing went unreported in the Irish newspapers. His eldest son, who had served as officer in the British Army in the First World War, settled in England. With his death in 1935 no. 2 was sold.[96]

CONCLUSION

Occupants of Day Place, due to their social status, inevitably found themselves members of the machinery of unreformed local government. A small clique of propertied men, sharing the same paternalistic views and unashamedly promoting their friends and relatives, took on what they saw as their duty.

As the transition was made to newer bodies with more representative memberships, an element of competition appeared. The self-made Catholic merchant, shopkeeper and publican started to occupy both the seats on the local boards and the town houses of Day Place. The change was largely without friction. The new moneyed class slotted into the system seamlessly. Except on religious issues or loyalty to the union, there was little to distinguish them. There were public servants and there were fraudsters, there were spendthrifts and there were prudent professionals on both sides of the divide. They were united by ambition and the status that Day Place gave them, if only for a while.

# Conclusion

At the beginning of the nineteenth century the town of Tralee was not thriving. It had a constricted medieval street plan full of crude cabins and rivers that ran close beside and sometimes into the houses. As the seat of the county assizes it burst into life twice a year, after which it returned to its role as a disorganized market town. The Denny baronets, patrons of the borough, tired of the town. They moved to England and demolished their castle in the centre of Tralee. Junior members of the Denny family were left to administer their estates and fill the clerical posts in the established church that were in their gift. The borough corporation was an ineffective closed shop.

It was therefore a bold move for Justice Robert Day to obtain a parcel of land on the edge of the town, divide it into building plots and create a terrace of town houses of a uniform elegant design, unlike anything seen in Tralee before. While it took a few years for the plots to be sold and the houses to be built, he found willing buyers. The tenants were a mixture of members of landed gentry or their widows, prominent barristers and medical men. These included members of the O'Connell and McGillycuddy families and Catholic professionals who were flourishing in the recently United Kingdom of Great Britain and Ireland. The houses were large, exclusive and fashionable and the householders were the wealthy Tralee establishment at the height of the Napoleonic Wars.

With the ending of war there was an alteration in the economy of the surrounding countryside while the port of Blennerville was developed for the export of agricultural produce. New arrivals to Day Place reflected this as the merchant class appeared in the terrace. The conversion of no. 1 to a post office and printing works in about 1818/19 was the first change from domestic to commercial use.

By the 1830s the number of merchants in Day Place increased with the growth of large milling and shipping enterprises. The new arrivals were the paternalistic heads of industrial businesses and employed men in unheard of numbers. By the 1850s they were leaving for detached villas in extensive grounds in the coastal region of Spa and The Kerries some 5–6km from Tralee, or the new suburb of Oakpark, on the northern edge of the town. They were replaced by merchants of a different kind: owners of the new shops and department stores being built in the town centre. The managers of these businesses also appeared in the 1870s. This commercial class was overwhelmingly Catholic and Nationalist, and a resurgent Catholic church made itself felt with the construction of Holy Cross Church at the end of the terrace, a reminder of the growing status and authority of the Catholic church in Irish society.

Local government began to be reformed and democratized from the 1840s and Day Place residents, on either side of the repeal/union divide, were leading figures in the new institutions. The Famine and land wars barely affected the householders except in their role as justices of the peace, poor-law guardians or organizers of relief committees.

As the nineteenth century turned into the twentieth, the gentry vanished from the terrace. It became the preserve of professionals, business owners, salaried police officers and resident magistrates. One house became a clubhouse while the lower floors of others were turned into solicitors' offices or doctors' consulting rooms. The denizens of the terrace now reflected the consolidation of the professional middle classes in Ireland as the tide went out on landlordism.

In the revolutionary period Day Place survived unscathed as Tralee was besieged and partially burnt by crown forces. Independence saw no dramatic changes at Day Place. The drift from residential to institutional use of the houses continued. Those that were still occupied at night were the family homes of the industrious self-made business classes with small family firms. By 1930 two houses were clubs, one was a doctor's surgery, one a solicitor's offices. The owners of a bacon-curing plant, a shoe shop and a wine-and-spirits warehouse made their homes there. The Dominican order had purchased no. 10 as an adjunct to the priory.

A whirlwind of change has altered the appearance of most of Tralee and swept away Day's Ireland. Day Place, however, is a constant. The façades of the ten houses in the street that bears his name would still be recognizable to Mr Justice Robert Day. Despite renaming of streets, his name still appears carved in limestone at the entrance to Day Place. Despite decades of neglect, a major restoration and conservation project is now underway. Despite being overlooked in local histories, the householders of Day Place can be rediscovered. Neither republican heroes nor tyrannical landlords, they have barely made the pages of history books.

Day Place remains aloof; a unique terrace of houses separated from the mainstream of the workaday town of Tralee. Its architecture echoes Dublin or Limerick while its iron railings divide it from the passing traffic and pedestrians. This enclave contained the *dramatis personae* of the story of a town going through a century of change, accommodating those at the apex of Tralee society. Without its construction, such a rich narrative could not have been written. As Robert Day's Latin motto put it, *sic itur ad astra* – such is the way to immortality.

# Appendix

A PARTIAL LIST OF OCCUPANTS OF DAY PLACE, c.1831–1931

This appendix is an attempt to list the occupiers of nos 1–10 Day Place over the period 1831–1931. It includes notes on the earliest occupants of the houses where this can be ascertained. Voters' lists from 1831 and 1834 survive and a directory from 1824 lists the principal inhabitants of Tralee including those at 'Day's-place'. These sources lack house numbers but examination of other documents such as memorials in the Registry of Deeds helps to clarify the picture.

The first full list of lessees is found on a map drawn in 1842. This shows the leaseholders from Revd E.F. Day, but these were not necessarily the tenants themselves. For example, businessman Peter Foley, who had much property around the town, was lessee of nos 8–10 but lived elsewhere. His two daughters inherited the property and continued to sublet the houses. Extracts from a series of maps carried out for the Denny estate in 1877 add to the information.[1] Mentions in local newspapers also help to establish a timeline. Announcements of births, marriages and deaths and auctions of leases and house contents give firm dates.

Griffith's Valuation was carried out in Tralee in 1850 and 1851. From that time a nearly complete list can be compiled using the revision books of the Valuation Office. The houses are identified by number and the tenant and immediate lessor given in each case. These documents generally list only the head of household, almost invariably a male, so other family members are not easily identified. Servants, which these large houses would have needed, are almost invisible.

The 1901 and 1911 census returns have survived and are available to view online via the National Archives of Ireland website, and this is the first time that we can see the entire members of a household. The 1926 census has yet to be released, so the final years rely on names in the revision books and newspapers, occasionally supplemented by documents that mention the tenants in passing.

**6.** The door of no. 10 Day Place in September 2020. The house has been abandoned. The original limestone door casing is in place, as is the fanlight. The brass door rapper and broken letterbox have been joined over the decades by a variety of locks and flaking coats of paint.

LIST

**Table 5. Occupants of no. 1**

| Years | Occupier | Notes | |
|---|---|---|---|
| By 1824–43 | John Busteed | See ch. 2. Part of building was post office and printing works | |
| 1854–8 | Sisters of Mercy | See ch. 2 | |
| 1860 | *Tralee Chronicle* | Printing works in part of building | |
| 1861–5 | Dominican Fathers | See ch. 2 | |
| 1865–85 | Edward C. O'Callaghan John Crosbie O'Callaghan | Edward C. O'Callaghan was a merchant and Town Commissioner. His name was replaced by that of John Crosbie O'Callaghan in 1877/8. The latter was a merchant who died at Day Place in 1884 aged 61 | |
| 1885–97 | Thomas Gibson | Property divided into house and spirit store | House |
| | Stack & Gibson[2] | | Wholesale Spirit Store |
| 1897–1906 | Intermediate and University School | See ch. 2 | |
| 1906–28 | Jeffers Institute | See ch. 2 | |
| 1928 | Honoria Healy | | |

**Table 6. Occupants of no. 2**

| Years | Occupier | Notes |
|---|---|---|
| 1831–46 | Charles George Fairfield | See ch. 3 |
| 1846–51 | Letitia Rowan | Fairfield's mother-in-law. Letitia Denny, daughter of Sir Barry Denny, 1st baronet, who married 23 Oct. 1799 William Rowan, counsellor at law and provost of Tralee, 1807–11. He died April 1826. She died May 1851 |
| 1851–61 | John Palmer | See ch. 2 |
| 1861–76 | Henrietta Palmer | |
| 1876–84 | Richard Elliot Palmer | |
| 1884–1931 | John Mary Harrington MD | See ch. 3 |

**Table 7. Occupants of no. 3**

| Years | Occupier | Notes |
|---|---|---|
| By 1808–32 | Captain Rickard O'Connell | Rickard O'Connell was adjutant of Kerry Militia and Daniel O'Connell's brother-in-law.[3] Died from cholera at Day Place in June 1832[4] |
| By 1836–47 | John Hurly Blennerhassett | Second child (eldest son) of Rowland Blennerhassett and Letitia Hurly, sometime residents of no. 6 |
| By 1851–74 | Lucy Slattery *with* Ferdinand Charles Panormo from 1862 | Lucy Slattery (1811–80) was a registered school mistress. Ferdinand Panormo (*c.*1824–81) was a bookseller and stationer who became Lucy's brother-in-law when he married her sister Catherine in 1861 |
| 1874–91 | Dr Michael and Mrs Lucy Lawlor | Michael Lawlor (1809–80) was married to Lucy Morphy who survived him, dying in 1891. His brother William, also a physician, lived at no. 8 |
| 1891–4 | Very Revd Thomas Moriarty | 1809–94. Dean of Ardfert from 1879, having previously been rector of Tralee, 1862–9 |
| 1895–1914 | James Molyneux Murphy | Solicitor, set up practice in Tralee in 1890 |
| 1914–19 | David Roche | Solicitor (1875–1942). Appears to have occupied house for duration of First World War |
| 1919–42 | James Molyneux Murphy | Returned to Day Place. Died 1942 |

**Table 8. Occupants of no. 4**

| Years | Occupier | Notes |
|---|---|---|
| 1803–33 | Daniel McGillycuddy | See ch. 3 |
| By 1833–82 | Daniel de Courcy McGillycuddy (senior) | |
| 1882–1901 | Daniel de Courcy McGillycuddy (junior) | |
| 1903–5 | Charles Paston Crane | Two successive resident magistrates for Tralee station. Crane wrote a memoir of his time as an RM.[5] Wynne was the last resident magistrate for Tralee, pensioned in Jan. 1921. Both were Oxford-educated sons of senior Church of England clergymen and RIC officers before becoming RMs |
| 1905–9 | Edward Melville Phillips Wynne | |
| 1909–37 | Joseph Augustus Slattery | Second generation of a family of bacon curers. Slattery's bacon factory was adjacent to Day Place |

**Table 9. Occupants of no. 5**

| Years | Occupier | Notes |
|---|---|---|
| By 1808–31 | Stephen Henry Rice | Assistant barrister for Kerry, 1799–1829. Died at Day Place June 1831 |
| 1831–48 | Walter Hussey | Leading supporter of Maurice O'Connell MP |
| 1848–53 | Robert Hickson | Excise officer and son of officer in 44th Foot from Sligo |
| By 1856–9/60 | Meliora Thompson | Widow of Thomas Blennerhassett Thompson, she was Meliora Mary Jane Young from Philpotstown, Co. Meath. Her husband had been son of Peter Thompson, treasurer of Tralee and captain in Kerry Militia, and died in 1853 |
| 1859/60 | George Day Stokes | County treasurer and magistrate. Later built Mounthawk House on the edge of Tralee, where he bred horses including a Grand National winner. Justice Robert Day was his great-uncle, hence middle name. His brother, Edward Day Stokes, was landlord of no. 7 |
| 1860–3 | Mrs Margaret Crosbie | |
| 1863–8 | VACANT | |
| 1868–75 | George Day Stokes | See above |
| 1875–82 | Mary Barry | |
| 1882–8 | Michael B. Stokes | See ch. 1 |
| 1888–91 | John Moone | |
| 1891–1911 | James Coyle | Secretary of the county infirmary in nearby High Street and a former RIC constable[6] |
| 1912–36 | Liberal Registration Club | Founded in 1865 to support Nationalist parliamentary candidates, they previously had premises at The Mall and then The Square |

**Table 10. Occupants of no. 6**

| Years | Occupier | Notes |
|---|---|---|
| By 1831–55 | Rowland Blennerhassett (junior) and Letitia Blennerhassett | Fourth son of Sir Rowland Blennerhassett, 1st baronet. Born 1780. In 1808 he married Letitia Hurly. Rowland died at Day Place in April 1854 and Letitia died the following year |
| In 1856 | Alice (or Alicia) Blennerhassett | Daughter of the above, born 1817 |
| 1860–6 | Rowan Purdon MD | Son of Revd George Richard Purdon and Mary Blennerhassett and thus grandson of Rowland Blennerhassett junior. His uncle was also called Rowan Purdon and was also a doctor and lived at no. 10 Day Place, dying in 1837 |
| 1866–71 | William Denny DL | See ch. 3 |
| 1871–9 | Richard Latchford | See ch. 1 |
| 1879–80 | Vacant | |
| 1880–7 | Charles Edward Leahy | See ch. 3 |
| 1887–97 | Dennis Barrett | See ch. 1 |
| 1897–1908 | Mary Ann Barrett | |
| 1908–11 | Timothy Barrett | |
| 1911–19 | Vacant | Two attempts to auction house were unsuccessfully made |
| 1919–21 | Elizabeth Hill | Widow of William Hill, prominent businessman and Town Commissioner. She died at Day Place in May 1921 |
| 1921–5 | Ownership contested | |
| 1925– | Margaret Hayes | Remained in Hayes family before becoming headquarters of Fianna Fáil cumann |

**Table 11. Occupants of no. 7**

| Years | Occupier | Notes |
|---|---|---|
| By 1846–59 | Honoria Ponsonby | Honoria Wren, second wife of William Carrique Ponsonby, 1770–1831. He died at Crotto. In 1849 her daughter married son of Rowland Blennerhassett from no. 6 (next door). Her sister was Margaret Crosbie of no. 5 |
| 1859–72 | Jerome Quill | Leading magistrate and freemason. Also agent to Major General Berkeley Drummond and agent for West of England Assurance Company. Died Nov. 1872 |
| 1872–94 | Elizabeth Quill | Widow of Jerome Quill. Died 23 Jan. 1894 |
| 1894–6 | John FitzGerald Lynch | RM for Tralee station |
| 1896–7 | Vacant | |
| 1897–8 | William James Eagar | Agent for Hercules Fire & Life Company. Leading magistrate |
| 1898–1901 | Margaret Stokes | See ch. 1 |
| 1902–4 | Vacant | |
| 1904–6 | District Inspector R.I. Sullivan, RIC | Two successive district inspectors for Tralee District, RIC. Barracks were immediately opposite end of Day Place |
| 1906–8 | District Inspector Charles George Meredith RIC | |
| 1908–12 | Louis Daly | Senior Inspector of National Schools |
| 1912–19 | Elizabeth Hill | Moved to no. 6 in 1919 |
| 1919–20 | Vacant | |
| 1920– | John FitzGerald | Founder of John FitzGerald & Sons Ltd (later Guinness agents), wholesale spirit merchants and bonded store owners |

**Table 12. Occupants of no. 8**

| Years | Occupier | Notes |
|---|---|---|
| By 1846–55 | John Busteed | See ch. 2 |
| 1855–6 | Revd James Lee | Rector of Ballymacelligott. Died Aug. 1856 |
| 1856–9 | Vacant | |
| 1859–83 | Dr William H. Lawlor | Brother of Dr Michael Lawlor of no. 3. Died Aug. 1883 |
| 1883–4 | Vacant | |
| 1884–1907 | Charles John Morphy | Solicitor. Brother-in-law of Dr Michael Lawlor of no. 3. Crown Solicitor |
| 1907–10 | James William Steele | See ch. 1 |
| 1910–30 | John Walsh | See ch. 1 |

**Table 13. Occupants of no. 9**

| Years | Occupier | Notes |
|---|---|---|
| By 1831 | George Hilliard | At time of death in 1869, aged 90, Hilliard described as oldest JP in county. Also one of two surviving officers of 'old' militia, having been commissioned in 1807 |
| 1869–71 | Vacant | |
| 1871–83 | Daniel Sullivan | Grocer and wine-and-spirit dealer. Died Mar. 1883 |
| 1883–6 | Vacant | |
| 1886–7 | Major Lionel Henry Mocatta Levin | Officer of Yorkshire Regiment, then stationed at Ballymullen Barracks |
| 1887–90 | District Inspector Alexander Gambell, RIC | District Inspector for Tralee District, RIC 1886–90. Commandant of Phoenix Park Depot 1902–10[7] |
| 1890–7 | Vacant | |
| 1897–1900 | James O'Hara | |
| 1900– | Tralee Catholic Literary Society | See ch. 3 |

**Table 14. Occupants of no. 10**

| Years | Occupier | Notes |
|---|---|---|
| Until 1837 | Dr Rowan Purdon | |
| 1837–45 | Revd Edward Day | Rector of Killgobbin. Died Nov. 1845 |
| 1845–55 | Deborah Day | Widow of Revd Day |
| 1859–60 | St Mary's Seminary | See ch. 2 |
| 1860 | Vacant | |
| 1860–1 | Captain Robert D Hay | Immigration control officer, Tralee |
| 1861 | David O'Connor | Draper with large business on The Mall |
| 1861–75 | Dr Thomas Duckett Maybury | Surgeon-Major to the Kerry Militia |
| 1875–80 | Francis Chute | |
| 1880–5 | John P Dooley | See ch. 1 |
| 1885–8 | Vacant | |
| 1888–90 | James Hoffman | See ch. 1 |
| 1890–1 | Vacant | |
| 1891–5 | James Ashe Conroy | |
| 1895–1905 | James Murphy | |
| 1905–7 | Agnes Walsh | Widow of John S. Walsh, auctioneer, valuer and pawn-broker of The Square |
| 1907–9 | Vacant | |
| 1909–12 | Dr John Roche Hayes | County coroner. Died Feb. 1912 |
| 1912–41 | Frances Hayes | Unmarried daughter of Dr Hayes. Organist at Holy Cross Church. Died Jan. 1941 |

# Notes

## ABBREVIATIONS

| | |
|---|---|
| CLG | Company Limited by Guarantee |
| De G & Sm | De Gex & Smale's (Chancery Reports) |
| DL | Deputy Lieutenant |
| ER | English Reports |
| ESRO | East Sussex Record Office |
| GRO | General Register Office |
| HC | House of Commons |
| *JKAHS* | *Journal of the Kerry Archaeological and Historical Society* |
| JP | Justice of the Peace |
| KCL | Kerry County Library (Local Studies Department) |
| *KEP* | *Kerry Evening Post* |
| NAI | National Archives of Ireland |
| NLI | National Library of Ireland |
| RCB | Representative Church Body (Library) |
| RD | Registry of Deeds |
| RIA | Royal Irish Academy |
| RIC | Royal Irish Constabulary |
| RM | Resident Magistrate |
| TNA | The National Archives (London) |
| UCC | University College Cork |
| VO | Valuation Office |

INTRODUCTION

1 Charles Smith, *The ancient and present state of the county of Kerry* (Dublin, 1756).
2 RD, vol. 533, p. 255, Memorial 358656.
3 *KEP*, 20 Sept. 1845.
4 Cited in RD, vol. 823, pp 274–5, Memorial 554011.
5 Gareth O'Callaghan, *Day Place conservation report* (Cork, 2019), p. 11.

1. 'MANY OF THE DEALERS ARE WEALTHY'

1 H.D. Inglis, *Ireland in 1834: a journey throughout Ireland, during the spring, summer and autumn of 1834* (London, 1835), vol. i, p. 260.
2 Benjamin Pitts Capper, *A topographical dictionary of the United Kingdom* (London, 1808), vol. ii (no pagination).
3 Inglis, *Ireland in 1834*, vol. i, p. 259.
4 *Holden's annual London and country directory* (London, 1811), vol. iii (no pagination).

5 *Pigot & Cos City of Dublin and Hibernian provincial directory* (1824), p. 313.
6 Inglis, *Ireland in 1834*, vol. i, p. 260.
7 Samuel Lewis, *A topographical dictionary of Ireland* (London, 1837), vol. ii, p. 641.
8 *KEP*, 25 May 1831.
9 *KEP*, 2 Apr. 1831, 8 Aug., 17, 28 Nov. 1832.
10 *Abstract of answers and returns, pursuant to act 55 Geo. 3, for taking an account of the population of Ireland in 1821*, p. 181, HC 1824 (36), xiv; Lewis, *Topographical dictionary*, i, p. 212.
11 9 Geo. IV, c. 118.
12 Russell McMorran and Maurice O'Keeffe, *A pictorial history of Tralee* (Tralee, 2005), p. 87.
13 *The parliamentary gazetteer of Ireland* (Dublin, 1844), vol. x, p. 384.
14 *Irish Times*, 22 Oct. 1879.

15 *Pier and Harbour Orders Confirmation Act* (43 & 44 Vict.), c. lxxxv.

16 *Pier and Harbour Orders Confirmation (no. 2) Act* (51 Vict.), c. cxii.

17 NAI, OL/5/2825, *Valuation House Book, Town of Tralee, Book 5*, p. 39.

18 *Cork Examiner*, 28 Aug. 1848.

19 *Tralee Chronicle*, 28 Dec. 1860.

20 Lewis, *Topographical dictionary*, ii, p. 99.

21 *KEP*, 25 May 1853.

22 *Cork Examiner*, 31 Dec. 1860.

23 *Tralee Chronicle*, 28 Dec. 1860.

24 *Calendar of wills and administrations, 1858–1920*, 1861, p. 243.

25 *Slater's royal national commercial directory of Ireland* (Manchester and London, 1870), p. 229.

26 VO, *County of Kerry, barony of Trughanacmy, parish of Tralee, Revision Book, 1868–77*, p. 149.

27 *KEP*, 25 Nov. 1908.

28 *Tralee Chronicle*, 25 June 1878.

29 *Tralee Chronicle*, 16 Aug. 1878.

30 *Tralee Chronicle*, 4 Dec. 1877. He was nominated by Richard Latchford, one of his neighbours at Day Place.

31 *KEP*, 7 June 1882.

32 VO, *County of Kerry, barony of Trughanacmy, parish of Tralee, Revision Book, 1884–94*, p. 193.

33 See, for example, *KEP*, 4 Mar. 1855.

34 *KEP*, 15 Feb. 1893.

35 Ordnance Survey, *Historic 25-Inch*, Sheet KY037–09 (Dublin, 1895).

36 Walter Allen Knittle, *Early eighteenth-century palatine emigration* (Philadelphia, 1937), p. 303.

37 Vincent O'Mahoney, *Merchant princes: the remarkable story of Tralee's milling families* (Tralee, 2016), p. 71.

38 Ibid., p. 82.

39 *KEP*, 29 Sept. 1879.

40 *Dictionary of Irish architects*, 'Co. Kerry, Tralee, corn mill (R. Latchford)', www. dia.ie/works/view/12212/building/Co.+ Kerry,+Tralee,+Corn+Mill+(R.+Latchfo rd) (accessed 29 Nov. 2019).

41 *The Kerryman*, 27 Nov. 1981; O'Mahoney, *Merchant princes*, p. 133.

42 Ibid., p. 48.

43 *The Kerryman*, 5 May 1906; *KEP*, 15 July 1908.

44 *KEP*, 3 June 1908.

45 O'Mahoney, *Merchant princes*, p. 52.

46 *KEP*, 6 Nov. 1915.

47 Inglis, *Ireland in 1834*, i, p. 260.

48 Lewis, *Topographical dictionary*, ii, p. 641.

49 Arthur Blennerhassett Rowan, 'The antiquities of Tralee', *The Kerry Magazine*, 1:1 (1852), p. 2.

50 *Castle Street, Edward Street & environs architectural conservation area management plan* (Tralee, 2012), 4.3.1.

51 *KEP*, 5 Nov. 1881.

52 *Tralee Chronicle*, 17 Nov. 1854.

53 *Kerry Sentinel*, 13 June 1900.

54 *Cork Examiner*, 2 July 1867.

55 GRO, *Deaths, Tralee registration district*, fourth quarter 1878, vol. 5, p. 505.

56 GRO, *Marriages, Tralee registration district*, first quarter 1881, vol. 5, p. 556.

57 *Kerry Sentinel*, 13 June 1900.

58 *KEP*, 28 Nov. 1885, 17 Apr. 1886.

59 *KEP*, 6 June 1888.

60 *Kerry Sentinel*, 13 June 1900; GRO, *Deaths, Tralee registration district*, fourth quarter 1900, vol. 5, p. 673.

61 VO, *County of Kerry, barony of Trughanacmy, parish of Tralee, Revision Book, 1894–1905*, p. 229.

62 *Census of Ireland 1901*, county of Kerry, Tralee poor-law union, Tralee Urban DED, Day Place, Schedule 7.

63 GRO, *Deaths, Tralee registration district*, first quarter 1901, vol. 5, p. 435; *Kerry Weekly Reporter*, 4 Jan. 1902.

64 GRO, *Marriages, Tralee registration district*, third quarter 1878, vol. 5, p. 347.

65 *Cork Examiner*, 2 Dec. 1896.

66 GRO, *Deaths, Tralee registration district*, first quarter 1897, vol. 5, p. 399.

67 *KEP*, 31 Mar. 1897.

68 *Kerry People*, 12 May 1906.

69 'Belmont House, Cloghers, County Kerry', *National Inventory of Architectural Heritage*, www.buildingsofireland.ie/ buildings-search/building/21302912/ belmont-house-cloghers-county-kerry (accessed 31 Dec. 2019); 'House: Belmont', *NUI Galway Landed Estates Database*, http://landedestates.nuigalway. ie/LandedEstates/jsp/property-show. jsp?id=1902 (accessed 31 Dec. 2019).

70 *Census of Ireland 1911*, county of Kerry, Tralee poor-law union, Tralee Rural DED, Cloghers Townland, Schedule 7.

71 *The Kerryman*, 13 Feb. 1909.

72  *KEP*, 10 Mar. 1917; VO, *County of Kerry, union of Tralee, urban district of Tralee, Revision Book, 1914–30*, n.p.

73  *Kerry News*, 3 Dec. 1917.

74  *KEP*, 5 Nov. 1881.

75  VO, *County of Kerry, barony of Trughanacmy, parish of Tralee, Revision Book, 1877–84*, p. 148.

76  *KEP*, 28 Mar. 1885.

77  *KEP*, 22 Aug. 1885.

78  *KEP*, 5 Sept. 1885.

79  *KEP*, 2 Dec. 1885.

80  *Kerry Sentinel*, 25 May 1907.

81  VO, *County of Kerry, barony of Trughanacmy, parish of Tralee, Revision Book, 1884–94*, p. 194.

82  *Dublin, Cork and the south of Ireland: a literary, commercial and social review past and present; with a description of the leading mercantile houses and commercial enterprises* (London, 1892), p. 243.

83  *KEP*, 3 Mar. 1897.

84  VO, *County of Kerry, barony of Trughanacmy, parish of Tralee, Revision Book, 1884–94*, p. 194.

85  *Census of Ireland 1901*, county of Kerry, Tralee poor-law union, Tralee Urban DED, Cloon More Townland, Schedule 8.

86  *Census of Ireland 1911*, county of Kerry, Tralee poor-law union, Ballynahaglish DED, Ballymagogue Townland, Schedule 35.

2. DAY PLACE: RELIGIOUS AFFILIATION AND CONFLICT

1  E. Margaret Crawford, *Counting the people: a survey of the Irish censuses, 1813–1911* (Dublin, 2003), pp 59, 133.

2  *The national gazetteer: a topographical dictionary of the British islands compiled from the latest and best sources and illustrated with a complete county atlas and numerous maps*, vol. iii (London, 1868), pp 683–4; *Census of Ireland 1861, part iv: reports and tables relating to the religious professions, education and occupation of the people*, vol. i, HC 1863 [3204–III], lxi, p. 15.

3  *Census of Ireland 1871*: i, II [C 873–I], HC 1873, p. 516; *Census of Ireland 1881*: i, II [C 148], HC 1882, p. 516; *Census of Ireland 1891*: i, II [C 6567], HC 1892, xxxix, p. 516; *Census of Ireland 1901*: ii, III [Cd 1058], HC 1902, p. 146.

4  Pádraig de Brún, 'Tralee voters in 1831', *JKAHS*, no. 19 (1986), pp 73–9.

5  McMorran and O'Keeffe, *Pictorial history*, p. 72.

6  *Cork Examiner*, 17 July 1863.

7  M.F. Cusack, *A history of the kingdom of Kerry* (London, 1871), p. 422.

8  McMorran and O'Keeffe, *Pictorial history*, p. 72.

9  *KEP*, 24 May 1813.

10  *The Gentleman's Magazine and Historical Chronicle* (Jan.–June 1819), vol. 89, p. 283.

11  NLI, O'Connell papers, MS 13650, Mary O'Connell to Daniel O'Connell, 2 Dec. 1801 and 4 Aug. 1802.

12  *Cork Examiner*, 17 July 1863.

13  *London Gazette*, issue 16599, 2 May 1812, p. 832; *A list of the officers of the army and of the corps of royal marines* (London, 1821), p. 661.

14  *Return of persons in civil and military establishments holding two or more commissions, offices or pensions*, HC 1830 (479), xvii, 58.

15  *Abstract accounts of sum voted for printing proclamations in Ireland, 1818–20*, HC 1821 (705), xx, 44.

16  John Caillard Erck, *The ecclesiastical register, containing the names of the prelates, dignitaries and parochial clergy in Ireland; the denominations of their respective dignities and benefices: and exhibiting the progress made in providing churches, glebes and glebe-houses for each benefice* (Dublin, 1820), p. 87.

17  NAI, CSORP/1819/535, Letter from John Busteed, proprietor of *Kerry Evening Post*, concerning intended withdrawal of government patronage.

18  Ibid.

19  NAI CSORP/1819/535/2.

20  Thomas Webster, *A brief view of the London Hibernian Society* (London, 1828), pp 5–7.

21  John Ainsworth, 'Two letters from the Eneas McDonnell MSS (Maynooth College Library)', *Archivium Hibernicum*, 31 (1973), pp 99–100.

22  Ainsworth, 'Two letters', p. 100.

23  *Enniskillen Chronicle and Erne Packet*, 2 Dec. 1824.

24  *Dublin Morning Register*, 8 Feb. 1825.

25  *Dublin Morning Register*, 24 Apr. 1826.

26 *Roscommon and Leitrim Gazette*, 27 Jan. 1827.
27 *Tralee Mercury*, 24 Feb. 1830.
28 *Western Herald*, 6 May 1833.
29 *Western Herald*, 7 Oct. 1833.
30 *Tralee Mercury*, 16 Oct. 1833.
31 *The Pilot*, 14 Feb. 1834.
32 *Tralee Mercury*, 4 Nov. 1833.
33 *Tralee Mercury*, 27 July 1836; Daniel MacAfee, *The anatomy of popery* (Belfast, 1860), pp 52–3.
34 *KEP*, 27, 31 May 1837.
35 *The Vindicator*, 17 Oct. 1840; *Nenagh Chronicle*, 7 Nov. 1840.
36 RIA, MSS, papers, diaries etc. of Hon. Mr Justice Robert Day (1745–1841), 12/W/7, *Map of several tenements in the town of Tralee, the estate of the Revd Edward FitzGerald Day, surveyed February 1842 by James Bourke, C.E.*, Shelf Mark RR/ MC/4/4.
37 *KEP*, 18 Jan. 1843.
38 *Galway Vindicator*, 8 Feb. 1843.
39 *Slater's national commercial directory of Ireland 1846*, p. 321.
40 GRO, *Marriages, Dublin north registration district*, first quarter 1851, vol. 5, p. 36.
41 *KEP*, 11 Aug. 1855.
42 Moriarty was appointed coadjutor bishop of Kerry on 28 Apr. 1854. On the death of Bishop Cornelius Egan on 22 July 1856 he succeeded to the see: 'The Post-Reformation bishops of Kerry', *Kerry Archaeological Magazine*, 4:20 (1918), p. 271.
43 *Leaves from the annals of the Sisters of Mercy* (New York, 1888), vol. 1, pp 471–2.
44 Linde Lunney, 'Mulchinock, John', *Dictionary of Irish biography* (2015) (accessed 4 Feb. 2020), https://dib-cambridge-org.ucc.idm.oclc.org/ viewReadPage.do?articleId=a9785.
45 *Tralee Chronicle*, 17 Aug. 1858.
46 *Tralee Chronicle*, 24 Apr., 9 June 1860.
47 *Tralee Chronicle*, 27 July 1855.
48 *Tralee Chronicle*, 15 June 1855.
49 *KEP*, 27 June 1855.
50 *Tralee Chronicle*, 17 Aug. 1858.
51 *Tralee Chronicle*, 8 Mar. 1861.
52 *Tralee Chronicle*, 31 Jan. 1862; McMorran and O'Keeffe, *Pictorial history*, p. 110; VO, *County of Kerry, barony of Trughanacmy, parish of Tralee, Revision Book, 1861–62*, p. 144; 'Story of Holy Cross Church', *Tralee Dominicans*,

http://tralee.dominicans.ie/ (accessed 12 Feb. 2020).
53 *Tralee Chronicle*, 1 Aug. 1862.
54 *Tralee Chronicle*, 5 Aug. 1862.
55 *Cork Examiner*, 29 Sept. 1862.
56 Annie Rowan (1832–1913), daughter of Arthur Blennerhasset Rowan, archdeacon and antiquarian.
57 *KEP*, 28 Sept. 1895.
58 NAI OS/140/Tralee/1841, *Ordnance Survey manuscript town plan of Tralee, County Kerry*. Sheet 5 of 8.
59 *Tralee Chronicle*, 6 Sept. 1845.
60 *KEP*, 20 Sept. 1845.
61 *Limerick and Clare Examiner*, 27 July 1850; *Limerick Chronicle*, 14 Aug. 1850.
62 *Tralee Chronicle*, 28 Aug. 1863.
63 *KEP*, 29 Aug. 1863.
64 *Tralee Chronicle*, 1 Sept. 1863.
65 *KEP*, 5 Sept. 1863.
66 *Tralee Chronicle*, 9 Sept. 1863.
67 *KEP*, 9 Sept. 1863.
68 *KEP*, 12 Sept. 1863.
69 Ibid.
70 Ibid.
71 *Tralee Chronicle*, 15 Sept. 1863.
72 *KEP*, 19 Sept. 1863.
73 *Tralee Chronicle*, 3 Jan. 1865.
74 *KEP*, 4 Mar. 1865.
75 NAI, OL/5/2825, *Valuation house book, town of Tralee, Book 5*, p. 43.
76 *Tralee Chronicle*, 3 Jan. 1865.
77 *Report from the select committee on the Farmers' Estate Society (Ireland) Bill*, Minutes of evidence, p. 32, HC 1848 (535), xvii, 359.
78 There is an advertisement in the *Kerry Evening Post* for an auction of 'modern and fashionable household furniture, the property of Mr P.D. Jeffers, Denny Street, Tralee': *KEP*, 24 Feb. 1836.
79 *Freeman's Journal*, 1 May 1873.
80 *KEP*, 2 Sept. 1840.
81 *Tralee Chronicle*, 29 July 1853.
82 *Dublin Builder*, vol. xiii, no. 150, p. 72.
83 *Tralee Chronicle*, 21 Aug. 1866.
84 Ibid.
85 Ibid.
86 *Cork Examiner*, 5 May 1958.
87 *Tralee Chronicle*, 30 July 1867.
88 *Tralee Chronicle*, 30 Aug. 1867.
89 *Tralee Chronicle*, 25 Aug. 1871.
90 *Tralee Chronicle*, 15 Sept. 1871.

91 Ibid.

92 Ibid.

93 While the will itself was destroyed in 1922, a certified copy made in Oct. 1903 survives in a file of papers lodged with the chancery division of the high court of justice and is now in the National Library: NLI D.27,270. Photocopy of certified copy of the will of Patrick Jeffers, solicitor, of Dublin, in which provision is made for the setting up of a charity school in Tralee, afterwards known as The Jeffers Institute, 22 July 1871, also photocopies of associated papers, 1893–1906.

94 *KEP*, 3 May 1873.

95 *Freeman's Journal*, 8 May 1873.

96 *Cork Examiner*, 7 May 1873.

97 NLI D.27,270; *Freeman's Journal*, 8 May 1873.

98 PROI, 6a/B41 1873, 'Copy of will of Patrick D. Jeffers': photostat made 30 Oct. 1903 included in NLI D.27,270.

99 Intermediate Education (Ireland) Act 1878, 42 & 43 Vict., c. 42.

100 University Education (Ireland) Act 1879, 42 & 43 Vict., c. 65.

101 *KEP*, 10 Jan. 1891.

102 *KEP*, 20 Mar. 1897, 28 Feb. 1898.

103 *Census of Ireland 1901*, Form B1, house and building return, County Kerry, Tralee Urban DED, Day Place.

104 *Dublin Daily Express*, 24 Apr. 1906.

105 NLI D.27,270.

106 Ibid.

107 *The Kerryman*, 16 Dec. 1911.

108 *KEP*, 17 July 1912; VO, *Revision book, Tralee urban, Day Place, 1914–30*.

109 'Knocking the Jeffers Institute, December 1967', *The Kennelly Archive*, www.kennellyarchive.com/search-all/670346 (accessed 26 Feb. 2020). The Charities Regulator, 'Jeffers Trust', *Register of Charities*, www.charitiesregulator.ie/en/information-for-the-public/search-the-register-of-charities/charity-detail?srchstr=Jeffers&regid=20019655 (accessed 26 Feb. 2020).

3. FROM 'TORY POWER' TO THE 'FRIENDS OF THE PEOPLE'

1 First report of the commissioners appointed to inquire into the municipal corporations in Ireland, xxvii, i [23], HC 1835, i, 428.

2 Virginia Crossman, *Local government in nineteenth-century Ireland* (Belfast, 1994), p. 11.

3 Crossman, *Local government*, p. 15.

4 *Cork Daily and Southern Reporter*, 26 Aug. 1869.

5 1&2 Will. IV, c. 17, ss 4 & 5.

6 Crossman, *Local government*, p. 11.

7 Salaries of County Officers (Ireland) Act 1823, 4 Geo. IV, c. 43.

8 County Treasurers (Ireland) Act 1823, 4 Geo. IV, c. 33.

9 Grand Jury (Ireland) Act 1833, 3&4 Will. IV, c. 78.

10 Crossman, *Local government*, p. 37.

11 *KEP*, 8 Apr. 1899.

12 *KEP*, 12 Apr. 1899.

13 *KEP*, 8 Apr. 1899.

14 T.W. Moody, 'The Irish parliament under Elizabeth and James I: a general survey', *Proceedings of the Royal Irish Academy*, 45C (1939/40), pp 49, 54, 73.

15 Gerald O'Carroll, *The history of Tralee: its charter and governance* (Tralee, 2009), p. 57.

16 Lewis, *Topographical dictionary*, ii, p. 641.

17 *Report of the commissioners appointed to inquire into the municipal corporations in Ireland*, appendix, pt 1 (1835), vol. xxvii, pp 427–8.

18 *Kerry Examiner*, 20 Oct. 1840.

19 Public Health (Ireland) Act 1874, 37 & 38 Vict., c. 93.

20 Town Councils and Local Boards Act 1880, 43 Vict., c. 17.

21 M.P. Quirke, 'Centenary of local government', *Kerry Magazine*, 10 (1999), p. 6.

22 Bryan MacMahon, 'The early years of Tralee workhouse, 1840–5', *JKAHS*, 2nd ser., vol. 19 (2019), p. 6.

23 *KEP*, 15 Apr. 1840.

24 *(Ireland) The fifteenth report of the commissioners appointed to inquire into the duties, salaries and emoluments, of the officers, clerks and ministers of justice, in all temporal and ecclesiastical courts in Ireland. Office of sheriff* [310], HC 1826, xvii, 109.

25 *Chute's Western Herald*, 29 July 1830.

26 *Cork Examiner*, 4 Oct. 1882.

27 R.B. McDowell, 'The Irish courts of law, 1801–1914', *Irish Historical Studies*, 10:40 (Sept. 1957), p. 380.

28 RCB P470.15.1.